JOHANNES VAN DAM

Johannes van Dam is generally acclaimed as Holland's most prominent food writer and restaurant critic.
He is chairman of the Foundation SGB, and in that function guardian of the 'Gastronomische Bibliotheek,' an extensive international Gastronomic Library, collected by him in over thirty years and, combined with a similar library under the same aegis, now containing over 90.000 important gastronomic works, consulted by food writers, journalists and scholars from all over the world.

As a journalist Johannes van Dam contributes to the Amsterdam daily *Het Parool*, the Belgian daily *De Morgen*, the weekly magazine *Elsevier* and many other publications. His weekly restaurant reviews in *Het Parool* are both feared and revered. He has published many books on food and is currently preparing a history of Dutch gastronomy and a book on Holland's favourite snack, the croquette. In 2005, his voluminous *DeDikkeVanDam*, was reprinted five times in as many months (85000 copies in total).

Johannes van Dam was born in 1946; surrounded by his library and kitchen utensils – he is an accomplished cook himself – he lives and works in the heart of his native Amsterdam.

D0920750

Book publications:

Alles warm (Bzztôh, 1988)
Brunch (Bzztôh, 1989)
Alles moet op (Nijgh & Van Ditmar, 1992)
De 25 restaurants van Johannes van Dam (*Het Parool*, 1994)
De Tafel van Tien (Nijgh & Van Ditmar, 1997 – 'Best designed book 1997')
Lekker Amsterdam 1st ed. (Bas Lubberhuizen, 1998, new edition yearly)
Twee handen op een buik (Nijgh & Van Ditmar, 1998)
Play with your Pumpkins (Stewart, Tabori & Chang, 1998)
Kürbisköpfe (Nicolai, 1999)
La Citrouille d'Halloween (Ed. Hors Collection, 1999)
Spelen met pompoenen (Terra, 1999)
Eten is een ambacht (Nijgh & Van Ditmar, 2000)
Eet op! (Nijgh & Van Ditmar, 2002)
DeDikkeVanDam (Nijgh & Van Ditmar, 2005)
Delicious Amsterdam (Bas Lubberhuizen, 2006)
Koks & Keukenmeiden (Nijgh & Van Ditmar, 2006)
De Kleine Johannes (Nijgh & Van Ditmar, 2006)

Johannes van Dam
Delicious Amsterdam

With a Guide to Dutch Food

with the cooperation of
Joosje Noordhoek

UITGEVERIJ BAS LUBBERHUIZEN

DELICIOUS AMSTERDAM WAS PUBLISHED IN DECEMBER 2006

EDITED AND TRANSLATED BY RACHEL ESNER
GRAPHIC DESIGN ANNELIES FRÖLKE
TYPE SETTER AR NEDERHOF, AMSTERDAM
MAPS DAV STUDIO
PRINTING HOOIBERG, EPE

WWW.LUBBERHUIZEN.NL

© 2006 TEXT JOHANNES VAN DAM / UITGEVERIJ BAS LUBBERHUIZEN
© 2006 TRANSLATION RACHEL ESNER
© PHOTO COVER HOLLANDSE HOOGTE

ISBN 10 - 90 5937 058 9
ISBN 13 - 978 90 5937 058 6
NUR 440 / 504

DURING THE PRODUCTION AND PRINTING PROCESS OF THIS BOOK,
SOME OF THE INFORMATION MAY HAVE ALTERED.

CONTENTS

PREFACE

A chilly Saturday morning around a café table, me with a cappuccino, Johannes with his tea (and I do mean 'his': he brings it from home). My visit this time was not purely social. 'Johannes,' I said, 'I need to find marshmallows. Thanksgiving is coming and that means baked mashed sweet potatoes with marshmallows.'

And so began another food quest. We started with the nearest Dutch candy store, not in the expectation of success but simply to get the lay of the land. Dutch marshmallows, we soon found out, are multicolored, dense cylinders of petrified sugar syrup entirely unsuited to the dish I had in mind. (Naturally, my recipe requires plain, white, fluffy, American-style marshmallows or, at the very least, marshmallows that float.) We tried several similar stores, but the selection was identical from one to the next. As we worked our way down the Leidsestraat, Eichholtz, an import delicatessen, offered itself as a likely source—certainly they have saved the day on more than one such occasion. 'They should be in on Thursday,' reported the shopkeeper, but of course Thanksgiving falls on Thursday and what if their supplier failed to come through? 'Johannes,' I reminded him, fearful he did not fully appreciate the urgency of our task, 'No marshmallows, no baked mashed sweet potatoes. No baked mashed sweet potatoes, no Thanksgiving.'

Shops here close early on Saturday and time was running out. If you can't find marshmallows in Amsterdam on a Saturday you're not likely to find them on Sunday or, for that matter, Monday: specialty stores usually take those two days off. That left only two shopping days until Thanksgiving. I'll admit I was worried.

But nothing inspires Johannes so much as an unsolved puzzle and on Tuesday came a suggestion via email: try the Food Village, an import supermarket out at Schiphol airport. It seemed a long way to go for marshmallows, but it was a lot easier than actually getting on a plane. And indeed, there they were, bags and bags of 'Great American' brand. Not an authentic American mark, of course, but good enough: Thanksgiving was saved! And then a week later, in the postscript of another email: 'And did you know the American Book Centre has very good (but what do I know about it) real American marshmallows?' Next year I won't even have to make the trip to the airport.

Expats who are particular about their recipes are likely to run into this sort of problem quite often in Amsterdam. I am not someone who compromises easily and especially not where food is concerned. Being American, I bake with vanilla extract, not that peculiarly Dutch substitute, vanilla sugar. A club sandwich – an American invention, and arguably one of its greatest – should consist of turkey, bacon, lettuce, tomato, mayonnaise, and toast, with absolutely no hard-boiled egg, avocado, or any other gooey distraction. I insist on having my coffee with my dessert, not after as is typical in Dutch homes and restaurants. And so on.

Most of my Dutch friends respond to my questions about where I might find unadulterated club sandwiches and the like with comments about Americans' poor adaptive capabilities. Johannes does too, but he also sees the challenge in the matter, and I flatter myself that more than a few of his research excursions in this city have been prompted by one or another of my peculiar culinary requirements. Amazingly, he almost never fails. Crab paste. A kosher deli. A restaurant with tables set sufficiently far apart from one another that a private conversation may be had. And the marshmallows of course. Still, what is not there cannot be found: if you're looking for unfiltered sake, Philly-style pretzels, or a really excellent pizza, well, with this guide or without it you're not going to find them.

Nor has Johannes kept any of his finds from the reading public: he is a journalist by trade and a generous person by nature. He is also sharply critical: you won't find much in this guide that is not worthy of note. This is especially true of the restaurants, one area in which the newcomer can really use some guidance. I've joined Johannes on more than a few of his restaurant reviews and I am sorry to report that it is not often as pleasant an experience as you might expect, for one simple reason: a great many of Amsterdam's restaurants are just no good. Poor food, inattentive service, a noisy, crowded, poorly ventilated dining room, these are all common features in local dining establishments. That our reviewed meals are free isn't as much of a consolation as you might think: I'd rather pay for my own meal than eat a bad one *gratis*.

But there are some safe havens out there, and even some real delights; here you have them all together in one volume. We've had some adventures finding them, and I hope you have as many more enjoying them. *Eet smakelijk.*

A.T. Shuldiner, Amsterdam, May 2006

DUTCH FESTIVE FOOD

The Netherlands don't have a reputation as a culinary paradise. It is an unjust image we share with our neighbors, the English, and with the Americans. But there is a saying in Dutch along the lines of 'unknown is unloved', and that certainly applies to our food. There may not be a Dutch *haute cuisine*, but we do have some foods that can make your mouth water.

The story of Dutch food is in a way a sad story, because if we had not had the huge culinary misadventure of the 1890's no one would have had cause to complain – except maybe the Belgians, who claim to have saved the classical French cuisine. This is particularly unfair, as until the end of the nineteenth century, Dutch and Belgian cuisine were one and the same – both lands forming one country until the Belgian revolution of 1830. The most famous Belgian cookbook, the *Volmaakte Belgische Keukenmeid* (1839), is even an almost exact copy of a similar Dutch cookbook of ninety years earlier.

But in 1890 a cohort of Dutch middle-class women devised a plan to ameliorate the culinary faculties of the lower classes, in order to promote better health. They set up schools (*huishoud-scholen*), where they proposed simplified, cheap versions of the dishes they knew best – the rich *cuisine bourgeoise* – as they thought that was the proper way to eat. Easy and affordable, this type of food now became available to the poor, but it ignored the fact that there are other qualities to eating than mere nourishment.

And matters only got worse. Those poor people for whom this mockery of 'decent' cookery was intended did not go to these schools; they had to work. Instead, classes were attended by the daughters of the middle class. Seduced by its inexpensiveness and simplicity (no rich sauces, no herbs, because they added nothing to the health, and taste was superfluous), they readily adopted this degenerated form of their own heritage. And so traditional Dutch cuisine was sacrificed and almost disappeared.

From that moment on, the link was broken between home experience and the *haute cuisine* of the restaurants. Chefs where motherless, as far as cooking was concerned. Restaurant fare suffered, as chefs no longer learned from an early age what good cooking encompassed, and there was a corresponding lack of critical customers. Only dishes from the so-called *volkskeuken* survived, and they did little to improve the culinary reputation of the Dutch. A sad story indeed.

So what is left of Dutch cuisine? Indeed, some things escaped the regime of the *huishoudschoolkolonels* – foods that were too deeply embedded in tradition or just plainly not part of everyday life.

The number three figures prominently at Dutch mealtimes. A proper dinner consists of three courses: a starter, main course, and dessert. The main course always consists of three parts – potatoes, vegetables, and meat. The order here is not arbitrary. As Van Gogh graphically portrayed, the Dutch are potato eaters, but they are also vegetable eaters. (In the Takeawaylands the potato is not counted as a vegetable, nor is salad.) In the old days, if you asked what was for dinner, the reply would inevitably be Brussels sprouts or spinach or carrots. Given the climate, their work and the soil, the Dutch have always been sober consumers of hearty, substantial fare. The country's religion, too, demanded moderation. Perhaps this is why we sometimes go food-crazy here, especially at the end of the year. Suddenly we are allowed to break with the everyday kind of dish and get down to some rich eating, partaking of all those things that made the *huishoudschool* teachers shudder.

It all starts with New Year's Eve. All new things have to be inaugurated in party style, preferably with a well-laden table symbolizing the good things people hope for in the coming year. On New Year's Eve you will still find in many kitchens large bowls of batter and spitting-hot oil, all ready for the preparation of traditional *oliebollen* (doughnut balls), *appelflappen* (apple turnovers) and *appelbeignets* (apple fritters). Eating *oliebollen* is more or less a national custom on the last day of the year, but the provinces also have an infinite variety of local specialties, such as *duivekaters* (specially shaped yeast bread), *spekkendikken* ('bacon fatties', a kind of waffle), *oude wijven* (literally 'old ladies'), and New

Year's cakes, waffles and rolls in many forms and flavors. Although the deeper meaning behind all these traditional treats has been forgotten, they are still eaten with gusto.

Among traditional 'farmhouse' specialties being revived today is a substantial pudding called *balkenbrij* (scrapple). Often sweetened with raisins, it is cooked in stock, cooled, then cut into thick slices and crisped in sizzling bacon fat. Eating *balkenbrij* was a traditional way of rounding off the autumn slaughtering season, along with other seasonal dishes such as *bloedworst* (blood sausage), *hoofdkaas* (head cheese), *zwoerdmaag* (pork belly), *rolpens* (minced meat in tripe) and *kaantjeskoekjes* (crackling).

A real party, especially for children, takes place on December 5 (Sinterklaas). Although Saint Nicholas's birthday is officially December 6, the Dutch follow Catholic tradition and celebrate it the evening before with special delicacies. The most traditional is *speculaas*, a spicy crisp cookie. When turned out, the cookie is a mirror image of the form in which it is made, which probably accounts for its name – *speculum* being the Latin word for reflection. Larger cookies are made in the same way, but from a different kind of dough known as *taai-taai* (literally tough-tough). This mixture of rye dough, honey, treacle, syrup and anise, is usually molded in traditional 'dolls'. A very old custom is the scattering of *strooigoed* for children to pick up. This consists of almost-round cookies made from fondant (*borstplaat*) and *peper-* or *kruidnootjes* (spice or gingerbread nuts). Marzipan is transformed into brightly colored fruits, animals and fairy-tale figures, but also realistic looking imitations of sausages, fried eggs, pieces of bacon and anything the baker can come up with. Letters made of chocolate are also traditional. A favorite drink on the evening is *bisschopswijn*, a flavored red wine, served hot.

But this is only the beginning. December is known as the festive month and Sinterklaas is just one of the major holidays. Until very recently, Christmas in Holland – unlike other countries – was not a time for exchanging gifts. But the giving of gifts, at least to grown-ups, has gradually shifted from Sinterklaas to Christmas, transforming the once exclusively religious celebration into a party. Although Christmas dinner was always rather more special than a Sunday meal, the Dutch are now going the whole hog. Truffles, goose liver paté, smoked salmon, game, and very good wine. The same has happened with traditional sweets. If the Dutch used to be satisfied during this essentially reflective, spiritual holiday with a few *kerstkransjes* (Christmas wreaths), made either of cake or fondant, they now search out all kinds of exotic sweetmeats from abroad. The English Christmas pudding *flambé* is now a firm favorite, along with German Christmas bread. Inventive confectioners have also developed a boterkrans, a variation of the Sinterklaas letter shaped like a Christmas wreath and decorated with candied fruit.

No one in Holland feels they should work on New Year's Eve – public transportation shuts down early, restaurants close, and even housewives take it easy. This is an evening of snacks and salads. The classic is the *huzarensla*, usually made with left-over pieces of soup meat, potatoes, pickled apples, vegetables – such as peas, carrots, silver onions, and gherkins – and mayonnaise – lots of mayonnaise. This dish generally shares pride of place with a herring salad mixed with freshly cooked beetroot. These simple, tasty and nutritious salads are now considered rather ordinary. Tables today groan under the weight of richer variations, such as Russian egg salad, and chiquer fish salads like shrimp, crab, lobster, and salmon. The Waldorf salad is another particular favorite with its decorative additions of walnut, mandarin orange and, occasionally, fresh pineapple. Once the Dutch get started, there is no stopping them. Festive Mexican bean salads, Asian rice salads, spicy chicken concoctions and French tongue salads, steak tartare, celery salads, and a vast range of fruit and curry dishes. Or there is filleted smoked eel, mackerel or whiting and new herring. And, in an old-fashioned home, there may be rollmops. Balancing out the table will be *kaassoesjes* (cheese puffs) or generous slices of liver sausage or *ossenworst* (finely chopped beef, sometimes smoked) with mustard relish. This is also the dip for a range of Dutch cheeses, diced into nibble-sized blocks or sharing a cocktail stick with pieces of preserved ginger, a gherkin, silver onions or pineapple. Sausage rolls will be warming in the oven along with the pastries, and French bread will be crisping. Oil will be spitting, ready for a variety of croquettes (for example, *bitterballen*), and there will be cheese soufflés and other delicacies that are generally made at home only once a year.

CHEESE ON BOARD

*K*aaskoppen – cheese heads – is the way the Dutch describe themselves – if they want to be modest. Long before the Dutch Dairy Board began to promote it with the help of the innocuous 'Juffrouw Antje,' cheese had been important to the Netherlands, as both a food and an export commodity.

These days, the product we usually export, and indeed the cheese the Dutch mainly produce, is Gouda, which is made from cow's milk, as is the equally well-known round Edam. But to think that things have always been like this is an error. In the Golden Age, Dutch cheese was usually made from sheep's milk, followed by cow as a second choice, and goat as a third.

Because of its hard structure, Dutch cheese is practical for export. Pressed cheeses are much easier to transport than soft cheeses like the French Camembert, which only gained notoriety when railroads began to connect the farms with the city – and when split wooden boxes began to be used to protect them. Hard Dutch cheeses need neither speed nor packaging, so the slow motion of the horse-drawn carriage and sailing ship was good enough.

In the Middle Ages, most products where distributed through markets, and in several cities these became quite specialized. For cheese these were Alkmaar, Edam, and Gouda, among others. Amsterdam was the largest consumer and export market. From the island of Texel came a very strong, green sheep's cheese, which was perfumed with a tea made from the animal's excrement and sold all over Europe for its peculiar qualities. In places where butter was made, the Dutch also produced low-fat cheeses that were distinguished from the full-fat varieties (and also made more palatable) by the addition of cumin or cloves (Leiden and Frisian cheese).

The success of Dutch cheese, then as now, was based on a few simple principles: all cheeses, cow or sheep, were of the hard, pressed type, which, after some ageing, keeps extremely well. As with herring, which was what really made the seventeenth century a Golden Age, cheese was certified. Buyers from all over the world knew that both Dutch herring and Dutch cheese were of excellent and durable quality. This made Dutch victuals a reliable commodity aboard ships, perfect for long journeys, and so the Dutch became a wealthy naval and commercial force. Dutch cheese was a staple in all the countries with which the Netherlands traded. To give an example of the importance of cheese on board ship from 1636: Dutch sailors had the right to one pound of cheese per week, while passengers were given twice that amount!

Underlying the certified production, marketing, export, and distribution was an intricate web of internal trade. Farmers sold their cheese to merchants, who in turn sold it at market, in cases where the farmers did not do it themselves. For small amounts, transportation between farm and market was by cart, but it was always easier to move bulk goods by ship. Thus, all markets were located near important waterways – and around all important markets grew cities, which became larger and larger. Dams were built to control the water, and many markets were held on top of the dams. They also gave their name to the emerging cities: Amsterdam, 'dam in the river Amstel'; Rotterdam, 'dam in the river Rotte'; etc.

Although cheese was the most important commodity, butter and milk where also briskly traded at the dairy markets. In the case of milk, the moment when the small ships arrived at the market was the most important for traders, as it was then that they were able to dilute it with water – for pure profit, of course. Although certification and control also existed for milk, the government allowed it to be diluted slightly so that the poor could afford it as well. The type of water used, however, was carefully specified – only water with a healthy provenance was allowed – as was the amount. If anything, this shows the typical Dutch leniency, paired with restraint and social conscience.

Large cheese traders took up residence near the markets of the big cities, and had their own fleet to transport their merchandise across the Zuiderzee and even farther abroad, for example to the Hanseatic towns.

At one time, even the French had to protect their famous and extensive cheese market against the commercial success of the Dutch: on September 18, 1779, the government published an 'Arrest du conseil d'État du Roi, qui interdit & prohibite jusqu'à nouvel ordre, l'entrée des Fromages de Nord-Hollande, dans le Royaume'; in other words: forbade the import of Dutch cheese! Commercial trade restrictions are very old indeed, and even the French king (in this case Louis XVI) was not beneath the practice.

Cheese remains an important export product for the Dutch, but these days foodstuffs are transported by train, truck, and plane. It is still the Dutch themselves who play an important role in the infrastructure of the world. With Rotterdam (the largest port of the world) and Amsterdam (with a major airport and still the world's main seaport for cocoa), the Dutch are well aware that their fleets of airplanes and trucks have simply taken over from the sailing ships that once made them into a world power of cheese heads. I guess they still are today.

DUTCH HERRING

No one ever gives it much thought, but without herring this country would not have had the rich history it boasts of today: no Golden Age, no colonies, no emergence of the important trading nation that even up to present still carries weight. It is no exaggeration to say that in days gone by the power now wielded by the oil sheikdoms was the prerogative of The Netherlands. The country was the finest supplier of the product that made distant travels possible: the herring.

Herring fishing is at least as old as the history of our country; herring was caught wherever it swum, but no one knew how to turn it to profit like the Dutch. Herring became one of the first products to come with a certificate: it had to meet high standards of quality, curing, and packaging in order to receive the government's seal of approval and enter the market. And so it came about that Dutch herring commanded – sight unseen – a manifold of the price of other kinds, as a longer shelf life was guaranteed. The Dutch profited mightily from this, and it is how they laid the foundation for their once-great empire. The silver from the sea gave them the Golden Age.

Eating *maatjes* ('mates') herring could well be the most important culinary tradition of our otherwise in this respect poorly endowed country. *Maatjes* herring is raw, but salted and fermented like many sausages and hams, and therefore undergoes a ripening process. Nowadays, all herring is frozen; there is no longer any great difference between the so-called green, i.e. freshly caught, herring and the older, 'regular' herring. This means that today there is little danger of encountering the feared '*traansmaak*' ('tear flavor') caused by oxidation.

But beware! If herring is not eaten (or vacuum packed and cooled) immediately after cleaning, the otherwise so healthy unsaturated fatty acids will oxidize, leaving behind this 'teary' taste.

In the past, people compensated for it by heaping on finely chopped onion, which, by the way, puts the fine herring flavor at a disadvantage. Today, onion is seen – quite mistakenly – as a gourmet condiment, and if you don't watch out you will undoubtedly be served it with your fish. It is unnecessary and even harmful! Good herring is ruined by onion! It is better to sprinkle the herring with a little fresh pepper, straight out of the mill; pepper will enhance the herring's flavor.

Eating the herring in pieces with a cocktail stick, as they do in Amsterdam, or holding the whole fish by the tail and biting pieces off, like in the rest of The Netherlands, is, however, a matter of personal preference.

A small note of caution: each city in The Netherlands has its own favorite type of herring; big or small, soft or meaty, salty or less so. In The Hague, for example, they like their herring small, soft, salty and with the tail on. Amsterdammers prefer theirs large, meaty, not overly salted, and served in pieces. And this is how I personally prefer to eat them, too.

HOT IN HOLLAND

As strange as it sounds, Asian cuisine was known in The Netherlands long before we could eat it in restaurants. That's not so surprising, really, considering how significant that area of the world had been for the country's history and economic growth. Ceylon and, above all, the Dutch East Indies (now Indonesia) were important colonies, which we exploited to the max. The same was true of all seafaring nations – the Portuguese, the Spanish, the English, and even the French – whose greatest interest was in spices and other non-perishable products. Some of these had already been introduced by the Romans, who had transported them over land; later came the Venetians and, with the rounding of the Cape of Good Hope by the Portuguese, many others, among them the Dutch.

Because it was considered chic to include Oriental foodstuffs on one's menu, slowly but surely more and more were imported into The Netherlands. Particularly in the 19th century, with improvements in the transportation of goods and people (steamboats, the Suez Canal, opened in 1869), products from overseas became increasingly popular. Many cookbooks, for example, mention *atjar*, often unrecognizably spelled but nonetheless referring to Indonesian pickled vegetables, which keep extremely well and were therefore much used aboard ship. Rice, too, was regularly enjoyed, and around 1900 there were quite a large number of Indonesian cookbooks on the market. Already in 1866 we find the *Oost-Indisch Kookboek*, published in Semarang and including Dutch and local specialties. This book was destined for use by the colonials. Many of them later returned home having acquired a taste for the east, and 1872 saw the publication of the extraordinarily charming *Indisch Kookboek* by G.G. Gallas Haak-Bastiaanse (reprinted four times in its first year and today available from Thieme Nijmegen, 1994).

This book initiated a real craze, with, as its highpoint, Catenius v.d. Meijden's *Nieuw Volledig Oost-Indisch Kookboek*, published in 1902 and encompassing 1,012 recipes 'with a brief appendix for Holland.' The later, revised edition included 1,381 recipes and was reprinted many times. Cookbooks about Indonesian cuisine are still a great success.

This was not, however, the case with restaurants, at least not at the outset. In a country where people preferred to eat at home, initially the number of Indonesian restaurants remained small, even though restaurant culture in general was on the rise. During the Depression before the war many establishments were opened by the Chinese, who continued to arrive in large numbers following Indonesian independence.

Thanks to their business acumen, strong family ties and social structure, the Chinese-run restaurant grew to become The Netherlands' most popular type of eatery. 'Doing Chinese' or Chinese takeaway was one of the few luxuries working families allowed themselves in the 1950s and 60s. Chinese places were cheap, and they demonstrated to the thrifty Dutch that there was fun to be had in eating outside the home; and besides: they were everywhere. Chinese families were large, and using a map of The Netherlands they could easily find cities and towns that were big enough and still had no Chinese restaurant. This meant that Chinese gastronomy – at least what the Dutch understood of it – was relatively widespread. One went to the Chinese to 'have a snack.' Noodle dishes and egg rolls were especially popular. The Chinese were careful, though, not to serve their guests real Chinese food, with its duck feet, fish entrails and so on. Or even real Indonesian food, for that matter; in the beginning, every Chinese restaurant was also Indonesian, commonly known as the 'Chin-Ind.'

Households with a genuine colonial background naturally looked down on these establishments. Only in locales where a grandmother was in charge or quality and authenticity were otherwise carefully supervised – particularly in The Hague, 'Garuda', for instance – were things somewhat better. Eating Indonesian, at least if you wanted authenticity, was something you did at home, which of course explains the flood of Indonesian cookbooks. Chinese food, on the other hand, was what you brought home from the takeaway. Cooking Chinese at home is thus a relatively recent phenomenon.

Because there isn't one single Indonesian cuisine – the regional differences are at least as great as those in Europe – every family had their favorite authors and cookbooks. People swore by Keijner or Steinmetz, Catenius or Oma Kaesberry – but rarely by Bep Vuyk, who was considered too 'Dutch'. Vuyk's work, though, was popular among the 'regular' (i.e. non-colonial) Dutch. Some cooks were unhappy with all these alternatives, and, in order to preserve their own traditions, created recipe books themselves or published recipes in magazines.

Being still interested in products and dishes that last a long time, the Dutch navy has also developed its own kind of Indonesian cooking. Despite the passing of the colonial era, this type of food has remained quite relevant for travelers.

RICETABLE

On the occasion of the Bicentennial in 1976, the Dutch government invited their American counterparts to a formal dinner at the Dutch Embassy. (Holland had been the first country to recognize the US!). Believing Dutch cuisine to be unworthy of such a celebration, they presented the Americans with that other 'typical Dutch meal', an Indonesian *rijsttafel.*

The *rijsttafel* was indeed a Dutch invention. In the 'barbaric' East Indies, dining around a table (*tafel*) was practically unknown. The colonials, seeking to uphold the traditional Judeo-Christian mealtime ritual, came up with the *rijsttafel*, an amalgam of many varied dishes with rice (*rijst*) as a staple, in order to have something to say 'grace' over. So say thanks to the Dutch colonists for this strange, inauthentic set up, for it still works today!

FUSION

It was only once we had become so rich and our families so small that it was no longer necessary to cook at home every day and that more interesting eateries began to be established. And because Chinese had perhaps become a little boring, it was the turn of the Thais. They began to steal customers from the 'Chin-Ind', and the whole gastronomic picture started to change. Chinese restaurants, especially in the big cities, began to specialize (often in name only) in various regional cuisines: Peking, Cantonese, Shanghai or Sichuan. The 'Ind' was now frequently dropped from the name. At the same time, small and large, often elegant Indonesian restaurants started to open. Following in their wake were places specializing in other types of Asian cooking: Korean, Japanese, Filipino, Malaysian, Vietnamese, Indian, Pakistani, Tibetan or Nepalese. And then there was fusion....

It was something of a revolution when in the late 1980s Jos Boomgaardt, known from his work at a French-oriented starred restaurant in Zuidlaren, gave up everything (fancy cooking in Drenthe was obviously not really economically feasible) to start a Thai restaurant in Amsterdam, which he later expanded with takeaway places around the city. He had certainly recognized the sign of the times, and found himself at the start of a whole new Asian wave.

Ten years later, when the increasingly popular Thai eateries in the city centers had definitively become the 'new Chinese' (including takeaway), Boomgaardt once again saw the light and transformed his Thai restaurant into a 'fusion' restaurant – Thai-French, or French-Thai. In this period, the late 1990s, this was the new international style. French cooking with an Asian influence, or the other way around. This was how they were cooking in the fashionable places in Asia's capitals, so that one found in Jakarta – even before it arrived here – 'new style' Indonesian cuisine, created by western chefs to please rich and spoiled tourists and businessmen, and to be able to sell their expensive wines.

Australia, with Asia at its back door, provided the model, and California, with its large Asian population and orientation towards the Pacific, did the same. Today, fusion is a style that appears to be here to stay.

In local restaurant guides, fusion has its own category with, for example, in Amsterdam, ten entries, some of which refer to themselves as 'eclectic.' The number of eateries where this sort of mixing is practiced, however, is probably many times higher. Sometimes the places are quite simple, an extension of the earlier Chinese or Thai; others are quite trendy and serve more expensive French cuisine with a Thai touch, such as The Dylan in Amsterdam, where a Dutch chef combines *foie gras* with lemongrass and flavors his pudding with banana leaf, colors it green and serves it with blackberry sauce – an excellent combination, although the banana leaf can be somewhat bitter.

COMBINATIONS

Many people are inclined to refer to fusion as 'confusion.' In a certain sense they're right, but they also often forget that some of the dishes we think of as traditionally Dutch or European actually have their origins in far-away places. We would be unable to create a balanced and tasty meal without 'exotic' products such as peppers, cloves, cinnamon or nutmeg. Even tomato ketchup, which we think of as archetypically western, is a blend of something Latin-American (the tomato) and something Asian (*koçsiap* is Chinese, and means brine of pickled fish).

And don't eggplants come from India? And how about rice? Tea? Even sugar, which we no longer seem to be able to live without, came originally from India. No one in their right mind would think of banning any of these from our kitchens – quite the contrary – and we certainly can't speak of 'confusion' in the case of these foodstuffs. But there's something else.

Restaurants use exotic ingredients such as ginger (which in the Middle Ages was commonly added to spinach, for example) or soy sauce and then go on to suggest that such dishes be accompanied by a good (and above all expensive) wine. This often destroys all sense of harmony. Ginger spoils the taste of wine, as do related spices, of which there are many. Soy sauce can have the same effect, to say nothing of too much pepper. A subtle scallop or bit of lobster will completely lose its character when subjected to Asian ingredients.

Modern, well-heeled urban dwellers like to lounge about in restaurants serving fusion cuisine, and to impair their already over-stimulated taste buds with dishes that are more like nuclear fusion than fusion – drinking wine all the way. In general, oriental ingredients don't work with western beverages; combining them is a waste of good wine, and good money.

Still, even Asian restaurants want to serve expensive wine – for the sake of profit, naturally – and some customers like to show off the size of their wallets. Although there are wines that work well (strong, sweetish white wines, for example), a Beaujolais or

Bordeaux will always lose out. Here, Europe is no doubt bested by Asia.

Other countries, too, came into contact with Asian cooking through their colonies, but with quite different results.

The British adopted Indian cuisine and are now addicted to curry and chicken vindaloo, particularly as a cheap snack after a night of beer drinking, while the French embraced Vietnamese food – their alternative to our Chinese (and, of course, the cuisines of Africa, where most of their colonies were). The Spanish and Portuguese, however, took quite a different approach. Although some of the ingredients they encountered were incorporated into their national cuisine, the most profound influence – particularly in the case of the Portuguese – was the other way around. The list of countries where this was the case is impressive: Madeira, the Azores, Guinea-Bissau, Cape Verde, Sao Tomé and Príncipe, Angola, Mozambique, Goa, Brazil, Malacca, East-Timor, and Macao. And this is only the beginning. Anyone wondering about the origins of Japanese tempura should know that it, too, was invented by the Portuguese. The Portuguese manner of frying in batter was also adopted by both the British (fish and chips) and the Dutch (the *lekkerbekje*, a piece of deep-fried fish). Influence was thus mutual. In Indonesia today, we still find dishes with a Dutch pedigree. We can even make a complete circle around the globe. Just think of the migration of vindaloo from India to England. It came to India via Goa, where it had arrived with the Portuguese, who made a dish including wine vinegar ('vin') and garlic ('alho').

Products and dishes have long been world travelers, and if we remain attentive and don't simply follow every new trend blindly, we will all get a lot of pleasure out of them.

FOOD AND DINING
IN AMSTERDAM

As a metropolis Amsterdam is certainly one of the smallest. It would be better to call it a metropolitan village, with its well under one million inhabitants. It is the capital of The Netherlands, but not the residence of the government or the Queen, although she is traditionally crowned there. The Queen and her ministers reside in The Hague. It is not the largest port (that is Rotterdam), and not even the place where the most important industries reside, like Philips or Shell. But Amsterdam is the cultural and historic center of The Netherlands, even the magic center of the world, as the anarchist Provo's from the roaring sixties stated.

That seems to be the role of Amsterdam in the world: a magical center, the center where al the trade routes of the Dutch Golden Age came together, where Rembrandt worked and lived and which was described by the famous French poet Baudelaire as the place where the air is permeated by the smell of eastern spices and where there is 'order and beauty, luxury, stillness, and sensuality'.

These days you can still find those things. It is the smell of fresh exotic herbs and spices, fruits and vegetables that permeates the air at the numerous food markets and specialized shops of Amsterdam. And the city now boasts over one thousand restaurants and other places where you can eat the dishes from all these foreign and familiar places, prepared from exotic as well as traditional local products.

The most comprehensive guide (the Amsterdam op Zak Agenda, a yearly publication that is a guide and a diary) sums up over fifty specialized restaurant sections.

The 15 restaurants filed under Dutch should be the most interesting for a foreign visitor – and for the Dutch as well, as they seem to prefer to forget their own culinary heritage. But wherever you eat Dutch food in a restaurant, one should always realize that real Dutch food is not exactly fit for eating in restaurants: the best Dutch food is served at home. But there are exceptions to the rule. One could try the De Roode Leeuw (Damrak 93-94), or the recently opened Greetje (Peperstraat 23).

Indonesian cuisine is almost considered Dutch. Amsterdam counts almost 50 Indonesian restaurants (called 'Indisch' or 'Indonesisch' here, reserving 'Indian' or 'Indiaas' for food from India!). Real lovers of Indonesian food now and then sneak to The Hague, city of governmental public servants, where also most of the former officials from our Indonesian colonies reside, so you can find the best Indonesian restaurants there.

The other restaurant categories reflect everything this modern society encompasses. Traditionally the Chinese were strong, like in any metropolis. There may be a slight decrease, but Amsterdam counts still over 130 Chinese places, now equaled by the amounts of Italian and French or French-style restaurants. In all three categories you will find expensive and sometimes excellent places, as well as simple takeaways and pizzeria's. Modern trends, like the Thai, the Japanese and, lately, the Mediterranean restaurants, abound here. The floods of immigrants, turning Amsterdam into a real international city, resulted in scores of Turkish (or Kurdistan), African, Latin-American, Spanish, Portuguese, Polish/Russian and even American and British and of course vegetarian places, although we still wait with baited breath for a German or Austrian restaurant.

Lovers of fast food can as a matter of cause find their trustworthy McDonald's and Burger King. Which brings us to the way the Dutch eat when they don't eat at home and don't indulge in the luxury of eating out in a restaurant. They go to the butcher or a specialized 'broodjeswinkel' where they can order a bread roll, stuffed with meats, cheese or salads, or with the famous Dutch croquette, a deep-fried crusty cylinder of ragout, prepared in over a hundred different ways. My favorites, with veal or these excellent small Dutch shrimps, the best in the world, are prepared by Patisserie Holtkamp (Vijzelgracht 15) and are also served at the excellent Grand Café Luxembourg (Spui 24). Famous are the beef croquettes at Broodjeswinkel Van Dobben and even the variety of the Automatiek Febo (a chain of 'automats') is not bad. The many hundreds of automats and 'snack bars', serving mainly deep fried food like croquettes and French fries (served here traditionally with mayonnaise, as observed with disgust by Amsterdam lover Quentin Tarantino in Pulp Fiction) manage to help the Dutch to stay their robust selves.

Only a few years ago 'The Foodie Handbook' stated that in Holland it was better for a foodie to take a picnic hamper than venture eating out. Foodies are now in for a surprise, and that surprise is called Amsterdam.

THE FLAVOR OF THE CITY

Back in the days when Albert Heijn – The Netherlands' largest supermarket chain – was nothing but a corner grocery in Zaandam, we ate what came from the farm and the market garden, food that had been processed, if at all, according to traditional methods. In those days everything tasted good, and like itself. Things were better in those days. Weren't they?

Then came the big bad manufacturers, and the big-time grocers who exploited the poor farmers, forced suppliers to consolidate, drove out traditional products, and left the small businessman penniless. We were in a fix. Seniors had to go miles to do their shopping, and the young mother's (or father's) unexpected trip to the drugstore to buy diapers became an expedition instead of a brief stroll down the street.

And today? Things are only getting worse. That may be true in small cities and villages and even in the suburbs, but in the city, it's a different story.

The city's taste buds have indeed been under threat, but that's nothing new. Even in the splendid Golden Age, the city fathers allowed milk to be diluted with water – otherwise it would have been too expensive for the poorer members of the community.

Tampering with food by adding all kinds of rubbish to increase the weight – and thus to raise the price – is a centuries-old practice. Swindle, falsification: we find it both in the small producer and the manufacturers, although with the latter we can be certain it's a matter of policy.

Everyone knows that manufacturers, with their bulk buying and processing of raw materials, can turn out their products far more cheaply than small-scale, traditional producers. No amount of adulteration can ever change that. And if you're products aren't *better*, in addition to being more expensive, then you're going to price yourself out of the market.

For decades it seemed that industry and chain stores had beaten out small businesses, traditional producers, and retailers.

But something was wrong in the brave new world of mass production. Animals became sick, harvests failed, bad things kept getting into our food… and although none of this was new, now everyone knew about it. This had to be the case, as we were all eating the same things.

Although real Dutchmen always calculate the costs first – only to then throw caution to the wind – after years of calculating, we have finally realized that, in the end, we're better off paying a little extra but eating well. This realization was slow in coming, but it has now more or less arrived. Although supermarket chains continue to open new branches – inhabitants of the Jordaan still mourn the loss of the excellent Lindeman shop, replaced by one of the better Albert Heijns, but no more than that – and although producers are still concentrated together, for a few years now there has been a counter-trend. In Amsterdam perhaps more than elsewhere. That's the flavor of the city...

City-dwellers were the first to be subjected to factory fare, and inhabitants of smaller towns and the countryside had a good laugh at the rubbish we called food. Today, however, it's the other way around. In the villages, the last tradesman has closed his doors, and now everyone goes shopping once a week at the supermarket, located somewhere far away. Where everything is neatly packaged and mass-produced, and full of E-numbers and additives. Perfectly preserved, it doesn't go bad so easily, but in point of fact it was never very *good* in the first place. Or it's nice looking and fresh – like the vegetables from The Greenery – but unripe and tasteless. Nowadays there are even country folk who prefer the stuff from the supermarket to things grown at home: they seem to find something strange in the fullness of the flavors!

In the city it's just the opposite. Tired of all the food scares and scandals, the attentive Amsterdammer has begun to seek out the small tradesman. This began some time ago with what used to be called 'reform' stores, which sold mainly dry goods – as dry as the people who shopped in them. Arriving with the 'provo's' and hippies in the 1960s were health food shops, where one could buy injudiciously handled but nonetheless unsprayed vegetables. These were the domain of the hippies and other so-called 'alternative' characters.

The growing popularity of these stores, but the often pathetic condition of the vegetables, which were more or less left to rot in their crates, led to the establishment of farmers' markets, where organic producers could bring their wares to the city once a week. These were a huge success. Following in the footsteps of the Noordermarkt, Amsterdam now has a market on Nieuwmarkt, and today more is sold than just fruit and vegetables alone.

One of the results is that the clientele for these markets has now extended well beyond the original 'green' devotees – in addition to the bohemians, art lovers and others always interested in good alternatives, one now finds yuppies and numerous other urbanites who are not only interested in maintaining their health and preserving the environment, but also in better quality and variety – and that's what you find at the farmers' market. In short, all kinds of Amsterdammers visit the Saturday markets, and because interest is growing, a whole new class of small-scale tradespeople have sprung up.

BREAD

Bakers, for example. For many years, Hartog was the one and only producer (baker) of healthy bread in Amsterdam. Then came 'hippie baker' Année, with his organic sourdough. These and a few others supplied the right-thinking Amsterdammer with his or her daily bread. But there arose a desire for more than both the mass-produced and regular bakery bread and its 'healthy' alternative. Places like the 'Bakkerswinkel,' 'Bakken met Passie,' and 'Crusts and Crumbs' opened, where bread is baked the old-fashioned way, with all sorts of goodies in it if you want, but also just plain delicious. At the farmers' market you can find stalls with bread from beyond our borders, baked by idealistic bakers, with something for everyone: Belgian *vloerbrood* (baked on the floor of the oven, rather than in a loaf pan), and bread made with pure wheat flour or mixed with rye – the latter stay fresh for a week, just enough to get you through to the next market day. In the meantime, Année has had to struggle with his conscience: his Dutch organic flour supplier was long ago swallowed up by a larger combine that has no idea what to do either with the product or this type of buyer.

Bakers like these have had to forget their lofty principles of using only 'home-grown' ingredients and look abroad – to France, for example, where organic bread flours are much easier to produce. Anyone wanting to continue using Dutch flour will only get ground between the millstones of the industry. Because nowadays organic food no longer means simply excessive chewing or whole-wheat almond-paste cake (as if sieved flour was suddenly poisonous) but also a certain amount of frivolity, anyone looking for authentic, rustic but nonetheless refined pastries and cakes can do no better than to stop by expat Scotswoman Stelle Robertson for shortbread or delicious Dundee cake, as well as other kinds of cake, cookies and pies. She also makes preserves.

FRUIT AND VEGETABLES

Greengrocers who don't have a stand at the market and their own farm suppliers have a hard time of it. The auctions are all run by The Greenery, and they're not interested in organic produce. Moreover, it's quite difficult for a greengrocer to admit that some of the things he has on sale are poisonous by setting them next to alternatives. Some of these retailers have begun to feel the squeeze.

Faced with the power of the supermarkets and their contractors, the really basic places have been forced to give up. Only the more expensive stores – sometimes referred to as 'vegetable jewelers' – can afford to purchase high-priced products from special wholesalers. The current infrastructure makes life difficult for the small retailer trading in fruit and veg.

It's no wonder, then, that there are lines at the market stalls, where it's sometimes the farmer himself who takes your order, or a specialist in the organic trade who knows where to get his produce. Take, for example, the herbs sold by 'Het Blaauwe Huijs': no one can beat them for assortment or freshness.

As a dedicated foodie, I can hardly get enough. Instead of the selection becoming more limited, with pre-packaged produce in the refrigerator section, I can now buy several types of thyme, three sorts of fresh chives, bunches of beautiful, mature coriander (where the upper leaves look completely different from the lower ones). That used to be the norm, but nowadays the regular greengrocer has nothing but young, tasteless bunches.

Do the rounds of the market and you will discover more kinds of plums than you ever thought imaginable. The bunches of raw beets or leeks look so lovely, you might be tricked into thinking you were in paradise on earth.

In mid-September I always prepare a special meal with wild duck from the market's organic butcher, accompanied by a few ceps (from the mushroom stand) and braised with organic shallots, with, as an accompaniment, one of my favorite foods – one you won't find at any of the 'jewelers': turnip-rooted parsley, cultivated for its large, meaty root. Cut into cubes and simmered it is a fantastic, flavorful vegetable that goes perfectly with the distinctive flavor of the duck. The leaves are, of course, simply parsley, which one can use for everything. (The root is also delicious in casseroles and soup, in place of celery root.)

SPECIALTY STORES

The nice thing is that you can now find choice products on every day of the week, and at other venues besides the farmers' market. There are, for example, a number of olive oil stores: Manfred Meeuwig & Zn., Olivaria, etc. Good cheese is no longer a rarity, and the same goes for wine. Outside the city center, there are places like Erik's, on Beukenplein, where the owners have spared no pains to bring delicious cheese, wine, oils, sliced cold meats and more from the country to the city (traveling as far as Sardinia in at least one case). Elsewhere, too, fine food shops have sprung up – more original than the types of places I remember from my childhood (Lebbing, Verstrijden, Dikker & Thijs) and which I had missed for so long – as have regular grocers where you can buy legumes by the pound and all kinds of other essential things.

What has happened is simply this: supermarkets have killed off those stores that worked at the most basic and cheapest level, but because Albert Heijn never has been, and never will be, able to serve the higher segments of the market, a huge gap was created, and it is this gap that the new, small-sized business have come to fill. It is not exclusively either a 'green' or 'alternative' market, or a market only for a wealthy elite and gourmets, who are always on the lookout for the best. These markets are now *one* market.

There is only one health food store that has retained its hippie image, with an interior decked out in inferior timber. It is questionable whether or not one should be pleased about the streamlined 'Natuurwinkel' chain, where everything tends to look alike, but the anarchical nature of Amsterdam means that there will always be alternatives. It is precisely the city that has managed to serve the new, more conscious, multi-denominational consumer. Nowadays, you buy your tea and coffee not in the supermarket, but at Lévelt or one of the other specialists, whose numbers are continually growing. Butter, cheese, eggs – the choice has never been so extensive, and the quality, if you know how to look, has never been so good.

MEAT

And the butcher? There are still plenty of 'pennies per pound' deals and, of course, the supermarket, where you can occasionally buy a piece of organic meat; but the biggest mistake one can make, as more and more people are realizing, is to buy cheap meat.

With meat, cheap always means bad – bad for the animals and bad for people. One can still eat meat, but we should eat less of it and better quality. There are the Groene Slagers, which, unfortunately, work according to an unsound system whereby their meat products, which by necessity come from a central warehouse, are lovelessly and unprofessionally prepared. Then there are butchers like Siem van der Gragt (organic) or Fred de Leeuw (organic not in name but in fact), or the good, old-fashioned De Wit in Wakkerstraat (traditional), who still picks his own cattle from the fields.

If you look hard enough, you're bound to find, somewhere in your own neighborhood, far from the farmers' markets, a variety of addresses, where artisans ply their trade, refusing to give in to the supermarket Moloch. Support them!

AMSTERDAM SPECIALTIES

For a lecture given to a group interested in the history of Amsterdam, I decided not – as one might have expected – to provide a listing of old restaurants, but rather to do a little research into typical Amsterdam foods, or those named after the city, and into local eating habits. Some of these specialties are still well known, *Amsterdamse uien* (small pickled onions), for example. And for years, confectioner Beune has been making *Amsterdammertjes*, a kind of candy in the shape of the famous little posts lining the sidewalks along the city's canals.

Some products are not named after Amsterdam, but are associated with the city, in particular with the Jewish community, such as *ossenworst* (finely chopped beef, lightly smoked). Although their origins are not always Jewish, it was the Jews of Amsterdam who made sure certain culinary traditions were carried on. *Gemberbolus* (pastry filled with candied ginger) is one such traditional dish, as are fishcakes and perhaps even Dutch butter cake. The hot meat roll (*broodje warm vlees*) found in so many sandwich shops is also associated with Amsterdam, as is the *broodje halfom* (liver and corned beef), which elsewhere is made with ham and cheese.

Residents of Amsterdam eat their large, meaty herring cut into pieces, with slices of pickle and speared on a cocktail stick, while in the rest of the country one simply picks it up by the tail. Could our way of eating it have something to do with the pickle?

An *Amsterdammertje* that sadly has been more or less forgotten is the custom of giving away the last bit of *jenever* in the bottle, those few drops that don't quite make up a regular glass. There were barkeepers who knew how to limit the damage caused by this practice. Outside of Amsterdam we find another kind of *Amsterdammertje*: a beer glass with a capacity of three deciliters.

Residents of Amsterdam – many of them, anyway – were rich people with refined taste. For example, they very much prized lamb's lettuce that was not yet fully grown. The finest seed was sifted out, planted close together under glass, and harvested when young. Known when mature as *vet*, Dutch growers referred to the rounded baby leaf as *Amsterdams vet*. In Amsterdam itself, however, it was simply called lamb's lettuce. The regular, full-grown type, with its elongated leaves, thus needed a different name, and came to be called *ezelsoren* (donkey's ears). These sorts of subtleties are slowly but surely being lost.

Some people, on the other hand, do still know that the word *Amsterdammertje* can also be used to describe a certain size and shape of Gouda cheese. Other typical Amsterdam specialties, though, are on the brink of extinction. Nowadays, there are fewer and fewer butchers making Amsterdam liverwurst, which includes lardoons.

One probably would never guess it from their reputation today, but at one time Amsterdam's inhabitants were known by a culinary nickname: *koeketers* (gingerbread or cake eaters). Their stoical repartee was undoubtedly 'liever koeketers dan doodeters' ('Better a cake eater than a loafer'). Still, there is nothing that we actually call *Amsterdamse koek*. There are, however, quite a number of delicacies that originated in the city's bakeries: *koggetjes* (cogs, a kind of butter cookie); 'Amsterdam cake'; Amsterdam *korstjes* ('crusts,' made of rye flour and honey); Amsterdam pumpernickel; sweet rolls known as *luilakbollen* and a specially shaped yeast bread called a *duivekater* (these last two also found in the Zaanstreek); *secretariskoeken* (secretary cakes); *magere mannen* (literally: 'skinny men'); *rouwpeperkoeken*; and, according to the cookbook *Amsterdamse geveltjes*, cookies in the form of canal-house facades. The latter are probably apocryphal, and the recipe is equally unconvincing.

So it seems that in addition to the well-known *Weesper moppen, Arnhemse meisjes*, and *Haarlemmer Halletjes* – all regional varieties of baked goodies – there were plenty of tasty things from Amsterdam as well, but no baker who has found it worth his while to keep on making them, although we still have cookies that resemble cogs. Let's expand on these typical products for a while.

AMSTERDAM CAKE

No one seems to know exactly what 'Amsterdam cake' is, but it was invented by a certain Jac.A. Güth (*De moderne banketbakker*, 1910). The recipe is actually quite simple: make little lemon sponge cakes and allow them to cool in the pan. Using a fork, prick them all over, and pour on twice as much boiling hot butter as used for the batter, letting it disappear into the holes. Leave the cakes to cool again. You may need to reheat the mold slightly before turning them out. Hide the holes with some fondant icing. Rich, but unbelievably delicious!

AMSTERDAM CRUSTS

Few people today still know what *Amsterdamse korstjes* are. It seems quite strange that a whole bakery tradition could simply vanish, not just the *korstjes*, but an entire gamut of sweet goods.

Amsterdam imported flavored gingerbread from all over. A list of the sorts sold from the stalls at the city's Sinterklaas (Saint Nicholas Day) market might begin as follows: spice, anise, orange-peel, citron, barley, currant, raisin, almond (known as *mangelkoek*, a bastardization of the Dutch word for almond, *amandel*), crystallized fruit, syrup, honey, butter, as well as so-called *hijlikmakers* (a corruption of *huwelijksmaker* or matchmaker), and a whole series of untranslatable types like *benistekoek, keuningskoek, bagijnenkoek, claeskoek, kerskoek, jaepjeskoek, fonteinkoek*, etc. Sinterklaas was (and is) not only the patron saint of Amsterdam, but obviously also the patron saint of gingerbread. Following the Reformation, the city fathers sought to suppress anything that had to do with Catholicism, but in the case of Saint Nicholas they were entirely unsuccessful. Perhaps people were too addicted to bakery treats, even if they were no more special than *speculaas* (filled or otherwise), *taai-taai* or spice nuts (see 'Dutch Festive Food').

Instead of importing, Amsterdam was also known for its imitations of cake specialties from other regions of the country. This led to a number of conflicts, for example between the burgomasters of Amsterdam and Deventer, famous for its own honey gingerbread. Quite a lot of negotiation was necessary before peace could be declared – *Deventer koek*, after all, had to come from Deventer.

Koekhakken (literally 'cake hacking'), a game of skill whereby an ax is used to chop off pieces from a flat, tough piece of dough, was a favorite attraction at fairs until 1654, when it was banned by the municipal authorities, concerned about the many accidents that occurred. As a boy, I tried my hand at it at the Saint Nicholas Day Market in Alkmaar. It's not as easy as it sounds, and it is best to play it entirely for fun, as what you get to eat is hardly a treat.

Amsterdam gingerbread bakers, whatever sorts they made, always had a shop sign featuring a man stuffing a whole slice of the stuff into his mouth. There was, though, apparently no truly genuine Amsterdam *koek* of the same caliber as those listed above – i.e. a loaf made from rye flour (wheat flour was expensive!) – but there were *korstjes*.

Amsterdam *korstjes* lie somewhere between gingerbread and *taai-taai*: small, individually baked double rolls of dough, made, among other things, with honey.

In the 1950s there were plans to give this already rather unpopular snack a different shape – for example, that of a pretzel – in the hope of reawakening consumer interest, but the effort failed. Today, only bread bakers working entirely by hand and according to long-standing traditions, such as Hartog, still bother making them.

Amsterdam *korstjes* were apparently also given away as favors at children's birthday parties, where they were tied to the arm with string. This was the practice up until the Second World War, or so I heard from an older lady who remembered it well.

The *korstjes* available nowadays (for example, from Hartog), are paler – due to the addition of wheat flour – and are no longer flavored with honey but rather with anise. In other words: something completely different. Should you want to sample the old-fashioned kind – in professional quantities – you could try the following recipe from a baker's almanac: cook 1 kg honey and 1 kg glucose with 0.5 l water; mix with 2.5 kg rye flour and leave to rest for several days. Then mix with 1 kg honey, 0.3 kg soft brown sugar, some honey flavoring (particularly if using artificial honey), 30 grams of gingerbread spices, 30 grams of carbonate and 20 grams of ammonium (you can simply replace the last two ingredients with 50 grams of baking powder). Roll out immediately according to one of two methods: either make long rolls and lay them next to each other in pairs on the baking sheet and, once baked, cut them into double pieces of ± 8 cm each; in the alternative, make rolls of ± 18 cm (three weigh 100 grams) and double them back on themselves, cutting them at the curve. Brush with milk or egg to give a sheen, and sprinkle with browned starch when finished. Voilà: *Amsterdamse korstjes.*

AMSTERDAM LIVERWURST

Amsterdam liverwurst is more or less extinct, although the marzipan version produced for Sinterklaas in fact imitates it. Amsterdam liverwurst is liverwurst with lardoons. The smooth kind, without lardoons, which has now more or less conquered the territory, is known as *Haagse* or Hague liverwurst. The reason for its popularity is easily guessed: not because it's less fatty, but because adding the lardoons makes for more work. Amsterdam liverwurst is more labor intensive, and this is what one wants to avoid – the large-scale manufacturers in particular.

There are other fundamental differences between Amsterdam and Hague liverwurst. Although both are traditionally made from pork and beef liver, with the addition of offal such as tripe, head and stomach and, for cohesion, rind or gelatin, the proportions differ from one butcher to the next. More important are the differences in flavoring. Both naturally contain salt and pepper, saltpetre, ginger and mace, but the Amsterdam kind also includes cinammon and sugar, while Hague liverwurst may have onions, thyme, and clove. Substantial differences, then: the Amsterdam type is sweeter, while the Hague version is more spicy.

Of course, there are many other kinds of liverwurst as well. From Groningen, for example, with lots of cloves, or the Saxon type with fennel, cumin, cinnamon, and marjoram. If your butcher still makes Amsterdam liverwurst, though, cherish him and taste the difference.

DICTIONARY OF DUTCH DELICACIES

This dictionary does not contain restaurant fare, as there will be waiters present, willing and able to explain all. It does contain however a few important generic words like 'organic', 'unsalted' etc.

Names that are (almost) similar in English (like avocado) or have an obvious outlet (i.e. pizza, hamburger) are also omitted.

There are special sections for cold cuts (*vleeswaren**), cheese (*kaas**), milk (*melk**), sausage (*worst**), bread (*brood**) and traditional speciality sandwich fillings (*broodjes**).

The numbers behind the explanation or translation indicate in which location you may find the item in the numbered list of shops and other establishments that follows (**see page 61**). Delicacies with obvious selling places (drinks) have no numbers.

aal: young eel 30, 40, 59, 64

aalbes, rode/witte/zwarte: currant, red/white/black 29, 40, 59

aardappelsalade: potato salad 29, 59, 63

aardbei: strawberry 29, 40, 59

abraham: large baked image of father Abraham, traditional gift at reaching 50 for men 6

advocaat: custard-like alcoholic beverage made of eggs, sugar and *brandewijn** 24, 59

amandelbrood: thin and crisp *speculaas**-like cookie with almonds 6, 22

amandelbroodje: roll of puff pastry filled with *amandelspijs** 5, 21, 31, 59

amandelpers: almond and sugar paste 6, 17, 22, 43

amandelspeculaas: *speculaas** with almonds 5, 59

amandelspijs: almond and sugar paste (i.e. amandelpers*) with egg and lemon zest 6

amandeltong: tongue-shaped butter cookie topped with shaved almonds 6, 22

Amstel: Amsterdam's favourite beer brand (owned by Heineken)

amsterdammertje: 1. miniature chocolate traffic cone. 2. last, incomplete *borrel** from the bottle (traditionally free; also *Rotterdammertje* and *Schiedammertje*) 3. same as *vaasje** (30 cl), but not in Amsterdam

Amsterdamse ui: small pickled onions, coloured yellow with turmeric 22, 30, 59

anijsblokje: anise-flavoured sugar tablet 25, 59

anijsmelk: milk with anise flavour, by dissolving anise sugar (*anijsblokje**) in hot milk 35

ansjovis: anchovy 22, 40, 59, 64

appelbeignets: apple fritters 31, 44, 59

appelflap: a mixture of apple, raisins, and sugar wrapped in a triangle of (puff) pastry and either baked in a hot oven or deep-fried; an apple turnover 5, 21, 31

appelstroop: apple syrup 42, 59

appelstroop, rinse: apple syrup with added treacle 42, 59

appeltaart: apple pie 5, 6, 31, 59

Arnhemse meisjes: sugar glazed puff pastry cookie (Roald Dahl's favourite) 6, 59

augurk: gherkin, pickle 22, 59

azijn: vinegar 42, 59

bakbokking: lightly smoked herring, to be fried 30, 64

balkenbrij: a spicy 'pudding' made of buckwheat flour and scraps of meat and bacon, stock and (sometimes) raisins and apple, sliced and fried (like American scrapple or German Pannas) 22, 54

bamibal/bamischijf: breaded deep-fried snack of seasoned Chinese noodles 3

banketletter: letter shaped puff pastry filled with *amandel-spijs**, made for Sinterklaas (Dec. 5th) 6, 31, 59

banketspijs: surrogate *amandelspijs**, beans replacing almonds. A custom started in ww II, during distribution, but still used extensively in most factory made, cheap pastry 59

banketstaaf: straight roll of puff pastry filled with *amandel-spijs** (made for Christmas) 6, 31, 59

basterdsuiker, wit/geel/bruin: inverted sugar, white/yellow/brown, colours of the clinging treacle 59

Beerenburg: alcoholic bitters, originating in Amsterdam, now usually from Friesland

beignet: fritter 34, 44

berenhap/berenlul: elongated meatball, sliced, with onions and sauce or mustard 55

Berliner bol: deep-fried elongated plain *oliebol**, filled with jam, custard or cream 5

beschuit: zwieback, sliced and toasted special round buns 5, 59

biertje: glass of (pilsner) beer, lager

biogarde: variety of organic yoghurt 42, 59

biologisch: organic

biscuitje: general word for dry cookie, biscuit

bisschopswijn: a mulled red 'bishop's' wine flavoured with lemon and orange peel, spices, and sugar, served hot 13, 24

bitterballen: small croquettes (see *kroket**), usually ordered by portion (6 or 10) 13, 27

bittergarnituur: combination of snacks served with drinks, usually containing *leverworst**, *gekookte worst** or salami, cheese and sometimes *vlammetjes** and/or *bitterballen**. Also: *borrelgarnituur* 13, 27

bitterkoekje: macaroon 6, 59

bladerdeeg: puff pastry 59

blauwe bes: blueberry, not the wild continental *bosbes** (that has black juice) 29, 40

blik: tin

blikje: can

bloedworst: black pudding, blood sausage 22, 54

boerenjongens: raisins soaked in *brandewijn** 22, 24, 59

boerenmeisjes: dried apricots soaked in *brandewijn** 22, 24, 59

bokkenpoot: elongated, flat almond and egg pastry, filled with apricot jam, both ends dipped in chocolate 5, 6, 17, 59

bokking: usually a (hot-) smoked herring 30, 64

bolo: cake from Surinam

bonbon: filled chocolate 17, 22, 59

boomstam: tree-trunk shaped cake 6

borrelgarnituur: see *bittergarnituur** 13, 27

borreltje: glass of liquor, usually *jenever**

borst: breast 47, 54

borstplaat, harde: confectionery made from sugar and water (see also *fondant**) 6, 22, 56

borstplaat, zachte: confectionery made from sugar and milk or cream (*roomborstplaat*) 6, 22, 56

bosbes: wild blueberry with astringent and aromatic, purple-black juice 29, 40

Bossche bol: large cream-filled, chocolate coated choux 6

boter: butter; most Dutch will term margarine as butter too, so they have to call the real thing *roomboter* (cream butter) or *echte* (real) butter. Butter is usually unsalted 33, 59

boterbabbelaars: butter caramel candy, specialty from Zeeland 22, 56

botercake: Madeira cake made with butter 5, 59

boterham: slice of bread, sandwich 35

boterkoek: compact cake made of solid dough consisting of butter, sugar and flour, crusty like shortbread, but with a still soft centre 5, 6, 31, 59

boterkoekjes: assortment of cookies made with butter 5, 6, 31, 59

bout: leg 47, 54

braam: blackberry 29, 40

Brand: decent beer from Limburg (now also owned by Heineken)

brandewijn: unmalted distilled grain liquor, rather tasteless; also used for preserving (sometimes vanilla flavoured) 24

broeder/poffer: large traditional fry from yeast dough with currants and raisins

brood: bread 5, 42, 59

    allinson–: wholemeal bread without any additives, rather moist

    bolletjes: (round) rolls

    bruin–: brown bread

    casino–: soft bread (white or brown) with square slices for *tosti's** and sandwiches

    croissant: croissant

    galle (also **challe**): braided bread, Jewish

    grof: coarse

kadetje: soft white bun

kaiserbroodje: small round hard roll, German style

kerst–: for Christmas, with currants, raisins and *amandelpers**

kerststol: = *kerstbrood**

knip–: bread with one large cut lengthwise on top, so slices seem to have two ears

krentenbol: sweet bun of bread dough with raisins, currants and sometimes candied citron peel

krentenbrood: a loaf like a *krentenbol**, sometimes with *amandelspijs**

kwarkbol: curds bread

maanzaad–: white bread sprinkled with poppy seed (also small rolls)

maïs–: corn bread

meergranen–: bread with various grain varieties

melk–: white bread, made with milk, so it does not dry out over the weekend

oberlander: German sourdough bread

paas–: for Easter, with currants, raisins and *amandelpers**

panda–: rich multigrain bread

panne–: white bread with rounded top

pistolet: small French bread, submarine

puntje, hard/zacht: small, pointed roll, hard/soft

rogge–: usually dark pure rye bread, pumpernickel

Rotterdammer–: same as *knipbrood**

rozijnenweit: raisin bread

stok–: French bread, stick shaped

suiker–: bread baked from dough with sugar candy mixed in

tijger–: white bread with flaky crust

viergranen–: bread with four grains

vloer–: not baked in a tin

volkoren–: wholemeal bread

waldkorn–: brown, with whole grains

wit or witte–: white bread

zuurdesem–: sour dough

broodjes: rolls, with any filling; see also *kaas** (cheese), *worst** (sausage) and *vleeswaren** (cold cuts) 11, 27, 35, 39

   traditional fillings:

bal/gehaktbal: meatball, usually hot, sometimes with gravy and, optionally, mustard

ei–tomaat–met: egg, tomato and mayonnaise

eisalade (also: eiersalade): egg salad

glipper: meat and hard boiled egg

halfom: combination sandwich of *lever** and *pekelvlees** (see *vleeswaren**)

krab: usually surimi with mayonnaise; crab if you're lucky

overreden: (litt: roadkill) minced meat with ketchup

speciaal: *tartaar** with hard boiled egg and onions

tartaar: minced raw beef

(filet) americain: spread made of *tartaar** seasoned with spices and mayonnaise

tonijnsalade: tuna salad

vleessalade: meat salad

warm vlees: grilled pork or veal, sliced and hot, with gravy

zalm met: tinned salmon with mayonnaise/salmon salad

zalmsalade: salmon salad (usually tinned salmon + mayonnaise)

broodpudding: bread pudding

Brusselse kermis: sugar coated biscuit 5, 59

cacao: cocoa 59

cake: like Madeira cake, usually sponge cake, bread shaped and sliced like bread 5, 59

champignons: button mushrooms 29, 40, 59

chips: in Holland this stands for crisps; English chips are *friet** or *patat** in Dutch 59

chocolade, puur of bitter: dark chocolate 17, 59

chocoladepasta: chocolate spread 59

citroen: lemon 29, 40, 59

colaatje pils: smallest measure of beer: ± 18 cl

conserveermiddel: preservative

crème fraîche: slightly soured heavy/double cream 33, 42, 59

dadel: date (fruit) 29, 40, 43

datum: date (day)

Deventer koek: compact variety of gingerbread 2, 22

diepvries: deep-frozen

dierlijk vet: animal fat

Dommelsch: Limburg's favourite beer brand

doos: box

drabbelkoek: Frisian cake from deep fried 'dribbled' batter 6

drie–in–de–pan: small, thick pancake

drop: liquorice, a favourite Dutch sweet in hundreds of varieties 56, 59

duivekater: fine, sweet bread with egg and lemon zest, shaped like a shinbone 6

dùmke: thumb shaped, anise flavoured cookie (Friesland) 6

eend: duck 40, 47

ei (plur. eieren): egg 40, 59

elitehaver: rich mixture of nuts and raisins, without peanuts 43

Engelse drop: liquorice allsorts 56, 59

E–nummers: additives that are admitted in Europe, ordered by number

erwtensoep: thick, well filled Dutch pea soup, only during the cold months 11, 13, 35, 57

falafel: small spicy Middle Eastern snack made with chickpea flour 52

fijne tafelsuiker: finely granulated sugar 59

filet americain: see *broodjes** 11, 54, 59

fleer: soft waffle, flavoured with anise, in Staphorst at New Year

flensje: crepe, thin pancake 39, 48, 50

fles(–je): bottle

flikken: chocolate drops 17, 56

fluitje: small beer (flute-shaped glass, ± 21 cl)

fondant: confectionery from sugar, syrup and water 6, 22, 56

framboos: raspberry 29, 40

friet: French fries/chips, also *patat** 55

friet mét: fries/chips with mayonnaise or *frietsaus** 55

frietsaus: thin mayonnaise, especially for French fries/chips 55, 59

frikadel: deep-fried skinless sausage with dubious contents (very popular) 55

frites: French fries/chips 55

frou–frou: filled thin wafer-like cookie 5, 59

gaffelbitter: small tinned herring fillets with various flavours 22, 64

gans: goose 40, 47

ganzenlever: goose liver 22

garnalen, Hollandse or **Noordzee–**: small grey shrimps – the best (*Crangon crangon*) 40, 64

garnalenkroket: shrimp croquette 6, 27, 64

gebak: general term for pastry

gebakje: cake for one person

gehaktbal: meatball 11, 39

geit: goat, kid 54

geitenkaas: goat's cheese 22, 33, 40

gemberbolus: ginger filled sweet and soft pastry, resembling 'Chelsea bun' 6

gemberkoek: ginger topped *gevulde koek** 6

genever: *jenever**

gerookt: smoked

gerst: barley

gevuld: stuffed, filled

gevulde koek: large cookie filled with almond paste 5, 6

gezouten: salted

glühwein: see *bisschopswijn**

gombal: gumdrop 56, 59

gort: pearl barley 38, 59

groene peper: green pepper 22, 59

groenteflap: vegetable filled puff pastry, triangular turnover 21, 63

groentesoep: vegetable soup 50, 57, 59

Grolsch: favourite beer brand from the East of The Netherlands

Groninger koek: gingerbread with extra ginger 5, 59

gula jawa: palmtree sugar

Haagse hopjes: mocha caramel candy 22, 56

hagelslag, chocolade–: chocolate sprinkles 59

halfroom: thin cream 59

ham/kaas croissant: ham and cheese filled croissant 5, 21

hangop: drained yoghurt or buttermilk, curds

hapje: snack, bite

hard: hard

harde wener: crisp crust, usually like crumbly pastry

haring: always cured herring, fresh herring being usually un-available 30, 64

havermout: rolled oats 59

hazelnoot: hazelnut 43

Heineken: favourite beer brand of the less discerning

hoestmelange: mixture of liquorice as cough remedy 25, 56, 59

Hollandse nieuwe: young herring, raw and lightly cured, served without onions for connoisseurs, i.e. if it is not rancid. Onions take away the rancid taste of oxidized herring, but also the taste of the herring itself 30, 64

hommetjes en kuitjes: soft and hard roe, fried 30, 64

honing: honey 22, 43, 59

hoorntje: cone 32

houtsnip: 1. woodcock 2. sandwich with cheese and *roggebrood* (see *brood**) 3. snack of layered *roggebrood* and cheese

huiswijn: house wine

huzarensla: Russian salad 35, 39, 59

ijslolly: ice lolly/popsicle 59

inktvis: octopus, squid 40, 64

janhagel: cookie covered with white candy rocks 5, 59

jenever, jonge/oude (also **genever**): Dutch gin, roughly young and clear/matured and yellowish

jeneverbes: juniper berry

jodenkoeken: large sweet cookie, sold in tins or tubs 5

jus: 1. orange juice 2. gravy

kaas: cheese 22, 33, 40, 59

    Amsterdammer: small Gouda type, 6 kilo

    Beemsterkaas: cheese from the Beemster polder

    belegen: slightly matured

    blauwe: blue

    boeren–: farmers'

    commissie–: small Gouda type

    dieet–: diet cheese

    Doruvael: soft, aromatic cheese (red crust, raw milk, farm made)

Edammer: small, ball shaped cheese

extra belegen: extra matured

geiten–: goat's

geraspt: grated, shredded

gesneden: sliced

Goudse: Gouda cheese, large wheels, general classification

graskaas: first cheese from the new season in the pasture

jong belegen: slightly matured

jonge: young, soft, unmatured

Kernhem: soft, red crust (industrial)

komijne–: see Leidse

Leidse: lean, spiced with caraway

Limburger: strong, soft, white cheese

Maasdammer: Gouda type, sweet (industrial)

Maaslander: Gouda type (industrial)

magere: lean

mei–: white, fresh cheese

meshanger: soft Noord-Holland (rare)

Mon Chou: cream cheese

nagelkaas: lean, spiced with cloves (Friesland)

Oud Amsterdam: very mature Gouda type (industrial)

oude: matured, hard

overjarige: very old (over 1 year)

Purmerkaas: cheese from the Purmer polder

rauwmelkse: raw milk, unpasteurized

Reijpenaar: very old, (industrial)

Remeker: unpasteurized, farmers' cheese, Gouda type

Rommedou: strong Limburg cheese

room–: extra fat; also cream cheese

schapen–: sheep's

Sleutel–: Leidse, farmers, unpasteurized with special 'keys' brand

smeerkaas: cheese spread

smeltkaas: molten cheese

vegetarische: vegetarian (no calf rennet)

volvet: full-fat

kaas uit het vuistje: cheese as finger food

kaaskroket: cheese croquette 3, 27, 50

kaassoesjes: savoury choux filled with cheese cream 6

kaassoufflé: 1. a kind of cheese fritter 2. a cheese soufflé 55
kaasvlinder: crisp cheese cookie 6, 22, 59
kalf: veal 54
kaki: persimmon, sharon fruit 29, 40, 59
kalkoen: turkey 40, 47, 59
kaneel: cinnamon, nowadays regrettably also cassia (the inferior kind Americans call cinnamon) 59
kaneelstok: cinnamon bar 34, 56
kano: elongated little cake filled with *amandelspijs** 5, 59
kapperappeltjes: caper fruit 22, 40
kappertjes: capers 22, 40, 59
kastanje: chestnut 29, 40
kattentong: thin cookie, resembling a cat's tongue 6, 22
kers: 1. cherry 2. cress 29, 40
kerstkransjes: round Christmasbiscuits with a hole in the middle and decorated with candy 5, 59
ketjap, manis/asin: Indonesian soy sauce, sweet/salty 59
kibbeling: fried little pieces of cod 30, 64
kip: chicken 40, 47, 59
kippenboutje: chicken drumstick 40, 47, 59
kippenvleugel: chicken wing 40, 47, 59
kipsticks: chicken snack on sticks 55
klapbes: gooseberry 29, 40
kleingoed: differently shaped cookies from crumbly dough 6
kletskop: ± ginger snap 5, 6
kleurstof: colouring
kluif: knuckle, paw, bone etc. 54
knabbels: munchies
knäckebröd: rye crispbread 59
knijpertjes: thin waffles 22
knoflook: garlic 29, 40, 59
koekjes: cookies 5, 6, 59
koffie verkeerd: milky coffee 13, 35
koffiebroodje: Danish roll 5
koffiemelk: condensed milk to whiten coffee 59
koffieroom: light cream 59
koffietafel: lunch with sandwiches and coffee 35, 39
koggetje: cookie with specks of candy sugar 6, 22
kokkel: cockle 40, 64

Korenaer: *korenwijn** by Van Wees

korenwijn: matured Dutch *jenever**

koriander: cilantro, coriander 29, 40

krabbetjes: spareribs

krakeling: 8-shaped cookie made with various kinds of dough, sweet or salty 5, 59

kroepoek: shrimp cracker, Indonesian 22, 50, 59

kroket: croquette; a cylindrical fry, coated with breadcrumbs and usually filled with meat, chicken, cheese or shrimp ragout (Not Dutch, but a French invention from 1691) 3, 27, 50

kroketbroodje: puff pastry roll filled with a croquette

kruid: herb 29, 40, 59

kruidkoek: spicy gingerbread 5, 59

kruisbes: gooseberry 29, 40

kugel: Jewish dessert made with flour, sugar, fat and pears (exclusive Dutch variety)

kuiken: young chicken 47

kunstmatig: artificial

kwark: curd cheese 59

kwartel: quail 40, 47

lam: lamb 54

lange vinger: boudoir cookie, sponge finger, lady finger 5, 59

laurierblad: bay leaf 29, 42, 59

Leeuw: thin pilsner beer from the south of The Netherlands

lekkerbekje: battered deep fried fish fillet, usually whiting (like in fish and chips) 64

lemmetje: small lime 29, 40

leverworst uit het zuur: pickled liver sausage 30, 64

licht gezouten: lightly salted

limoen: lime 29, 40

linzenvlaai: fruit pie with crumbly dough like Linzer Torte, see *vlaai** 65

loempia: spring roll 50, 55, 59

lollie: lollypop 56, 59

Luikse wafel: wafer from Liège 22

luilakbol: hot small white buns, especially made for 'Luilak' (= lazy-bones, early Saturday before Pentecost) 5

mager: lean, low-fat

maïs: corn

makreel: mackerel 40, 64

mandarijn: mandarin, satsuma, tangerine 29, 40, 59

margarine: margarine, but most Dutch will stubbornly call this *boter** 59

marsepein: marzipan, made of almond and sugar, especially around Sinterklaas, in various shapes 5, 6, 59, 56

matse: Jewish unleavened Passover bread, water cracker 22, 59

maus: kale (regional)

meervoudig onverzadigd vet: polyunsaturated fat

melkchocolade: milk chocolate 17, 56, 59

melk: milk 59

boerenmelk: farmers' milk

chocolade–: chocolate milk

halfvolle: semi skimmed

karne–: buttermilk

koffie–: condensed milk to whiten coffee

magere: skimmed

volle: full-fat

mergbroodje: hot roll filled with marrow

mieriskwortel: horseradish 8, 22

mossel: mussel 40, 64

mosterd: mustard 22, 59

muisjes: sugar coated aniseed. *Beschuit** *met muisjes* is a treat at birth, blue for boys, pink for girls 5, 56, 59

muisjes, gestampte: powdered *muisjes** 22, 59

nagelhout: dried salted beef (like *Bündnerfleisch* or *bresaola*) from Eastern Netherlands

nagerecht: dessert

nasibal: large, spicy (Indonesian) rice croquette 3

negerzoen: cookie topped with large marshmellow, covered with chocolate 56, 59

nierbroodje: hot fritter with kidney ragout 6

nieuwjaarskoek: speciality cake for New Year

nieuwjaarswafels: waffle baked especially for New Year's Eve

noga: nougat 34, 56

Nutella: hazelnut and chocolate spread 59

oester, wilde: Portuguese oyster 40, 64

oester, Zeeuwse: flat oyster from Zeeland 40, 64

oesterzwam: oyster mushroom, pleurote 29, 40, 59

oliebollen: deep-fried yeasted dough balls, either plain or filled with currants, raisins, candied peel or diced apple 34, 44

olijven: olives 22, 40, 59

ongezouten: unsalted

ontbijt: breakfast

ontbijtkoek: gingerbread 5, 59

onverzadigd vet: unsaturated fat

Ooyevaer: *jenever** by Van Wees

oranjebitter: sweet orange liqueur, especially on Koninginnedag (Queen's Day, April 30th)

oranjekoek: large, orange glazed simple flat round cake (Friesland)

orgeadebolus: like *gemberbolus**, but with *amandelspijs**

oublie: thin wafer, rolled up and sometimes filled with cream 6, 34, 44

oude wijven: spongy biscuits with anise cut into the form of a woman 6, 22

ouwe: short for *oude jenever**, lightly aged, yellow coloured Dutch gin

paling, gerookte: smoked eel 40, 59, 64

palingbroodje: roll baked with eel inside

palmsuiker: palm sugar 22, 59

panharing: fried and pickled herring 30, 64

pannenkoek: large pancake 48

pannenkoekenstroop: pancake syrup

paprika: 1. bell pepper, sweet pepper 2. paprika 29, 40, 59

pasteitje, kippen–: chicken vol-au-vent 39, 50

patat: French fries/chips 55

patat mét: French fries/chips with mayonnaise 14, 55

pekel: brine

penséetaart: *amandelspijs** filled cake 5

pepermunt: mint 56, 59

pepernootjes (kruidnootjes): small round spicy biscuits for scattering on Sinterklaas (Dec. 5th) 5, 59

pijnboompitten: pine nuts 22, 40, 43

pijpje: small bottle of beer, usually 33 cl

pils: lager or pilsner beer, the most common beer in Holland

pilsje: glass of lager

pinda: peanut 43, 59

pindakaas: peanut butter 42, 59

pitmop: square cookie with almond on top (sweet or salty) 6

pittig: strong, pungent

plantaardig vet: vegetable fat

poedersuiker: powdered/icing sugar 59

poffertjes: small, lens shaped yeasted pancakes, served with butter and sugar and various other toppings 48

poot: leg 47, 54

praline: filled chocolate (Flemish) 17, 22

pruim, gedroogd: prune 43, 59

pruim: plum 29, 40, 59

pruimedant: prune 43, 59

puddingbroodje: soft white bun filled with custard 5

punt: wedge

radijs: radish 29, 40, 59

ragoutbroodje: puff pastry roll filled with ragout 6

rauw: raw

reep: bar, usually chocolate

rietsuiker: cane sugar 42, 59

rijst: rice

rissole: deep-fried, ragout filled rolled crepe

rivierkreeft: crayfish 40, 64

rode peper: red hot chilli pepper (= *Spaanse peper**) 29, 40, 59

roerbakken: stir-fry

rolmops: filleted pickled herring rolled around a gherkin and held in place with a cocktail stick 30, 64

roombroodje: soft white bun filled with custard (= *pudding-broodje* (see *brood**)) 5

roomijs: ice cream 32, 59

roti: savoury filled pancake (Surinam)

rotje: large crouton, usually filled

rotterdammertje: 1. small cocktail salami 2. = *amster-dammertje* 2*

roze peper: pink pepper 22

rozijn: raisin 43, 59

rucola: rocket, arugula 29, 40, 59

rund: beef 54

rundvleeskroket: a croquette with a minimum of 20% beef 3, 6, 27, 39

Russisch ei: a variation on Russian salad, with hard-boiled eggs, anchovies or sardines, capers, lettuce and gherkins 35, 39

sambal: hot pepper condiment from Indonesia (many varieties) 22, 59

sap: juice

sara: female *abraham** 6

saté: skewered meat, usually chicken (ajam), pork (babi) or lamb/goat (kambing), served with peanut sauce

saucijzenbroodje: hot sausage roll made with puff pastry 5, 31

schaap: sheep

scharrel–: free range

schelvislever: liver of haddock, eaten with toast as a snack 22, 64

schiedammertje: = *amsterdammertje* 2*

schnitzel: scallop, like veal scallop, cutlet

shoarma: pita bread filled with döner kebab, lamb (= halal) or pork with sauce and salad 52

sinaasappel: orange 29, 40, 59

sjalot: shallot 29, 40, 59

slagroom: double/heavy cream. Also: whipped cream

slagroompunt: wedge of whipped cream cake 6

slagroomsoesjes: choux filled with whipped cream 6

slagroomtruffel: cream and butter filled chocolate truffle 6, 17, 22

slakken: snails 40, 59, 64

slemp: traditional spiced drink

smaakstof: aromatic substance

smaakversterker: taste enhancer (MSG)

sneeuwbal: large, light plain *oliebol**, sliced and filled with whipped cream 5

snert: thick, richly filled pea soup, *erwtensoep** 11, 13, 35, 57

snoepje: candy

soepballetjes: forcemeat balls

sojasaus: soy sauce 22, 59

sorbet: 1. soft water ice, usually fruit flavoured 2. ice cream with fruits, whipped cream and fruit syrup 32, 50

Spa rood/blauw: mineral water, fizzy/plain

Spaanse peper: red hot chilli pepper (= *rode peper**) 29, 40, 59

speciaaltje: croquette shaped, seasoned meatball 3, 55

speculaas: crunchy sweet and spicy biscuit molded on a *speculaasplank*, a carved wooden mould representing symbolic or decorative figures, with or without almonds 5, 59

spekbokking: cold smoked herring, usually thinly sliced, like eel, fat bloater 30, 64

spekkendikken: cakes made of either rye or wheat flour, eggs, butter or suet and brown sugar or syrup and fried in an iron pan with a rasher of bacon or slice of sausage

spekkie: yellow & pink layered, lozenge shaped marshmallow 34, 56

spiering: smelt 40, 64

sprits, Utrechtse: variety of shortbread 5, 59

sprot: small fish rather like whitebait, smoked in bunches or filleted 30, 40, 64

stengel: savoury stick of puff pastry, with salt, almonds or cheese 6

stip: sauce (regional)

strooigoed: small biscuits or sweets used for scattering on Sinterklaas evening (Dec. 5th) 56, 59

stroop: syrup, treacle 59

stroopkoek: treacle cookie 5, 59

stroopwafel: treacle filled wafers 5, 22, 59

studentenhaver: mixture of nuts and raisins, also containing peanuts 43, 59

suiker: sugar

suiker, kristal–: granulated sugar

suikerarm: low sugar content

suikergoed: sugar figurines 5, 56

suikerklontje: lump/cube of sugar

suikerspin: candy floss/cotton candy 34

suikervrij: sugar free

suikerzakje: sugar bag
sukade: candied citron peel 22, 43

taai–taai: biscuit shaped like a large *speculaas** biscuit and made with spicy *taai* (= tough) dough of rye, honey syrup and anise 5, 59
taart: cake 5, 6, 59
taartje: small, individual cake
taartpunt: wedge of cake
tarwe: wheat
tasje: shopping bag
THT (**tenminste houdbaar tot**): best before
toetje: dessert
tofubroodje: vegetarian *saucijzenbroodje**, made with tofu 5, 42
tompoes (also: **tompouce**): yellow cream filled mille-feuille/napoleon 5, 31
tosti: grilled ham/cheese sandwich; other fillings possible 13
truffel: 1. truffle 2. chocolate truffle
tuinkers: garden cress 29, 40, 59
tulband: turban shaped fruitcake, Kugelhopf, high Bundt pan 6, 22
tulpje: tulip shaped beer glass, 22 cl
tumtum: mixed jelly candy 56

UCD (**uiterste consumptie datum**): can be used until…
uitsmijter: 2 or 3 slices of bread, filled with roast beef/ham, cheese etc., with 2 fried eggs on top – sunny side up. ½ *uitsmijter* = 2 slices + 1 egg. 14, 27, 39

vaasje: normal glass of beer (originally 30 cl, now usually 24 cl; some bars use 22 cl glasses!)
Van Wees, A: Amsterdam distiller of excellent *jenever** and other liquors
verzadigd vet: saturated fat
vetarm: low-fat
vetvrij: fat free
vietnammetjes: small, hot spring rolls (= *vlammetjes**) 13
vijg: fig 29, 43
viskoekje: fishcake 64

vla: custard 59

vlaai: flat fruitpie (sometimes with rice) made with bread dough (Limburg) 31, 65

vlammetjes: spicy hot small spring rolls 13

vlees: meat

vleeswaren: cold cuts. See also *worst** (sausage) 11, 22, 54, 59

  achterham: cured and boiled leg of pork, ham

  bacon: bacon

  casselerrib: smoked pork chop

  corned beef: tinned, pressed pieces of beef

  fricandeau, kalfs–/varkens–: roast meat, veal/pork

  gebraden gehakt: meat loaf

  hoofdkaas: a terrine of pig's head in a pork-based gelatine

  kalfsborst: (stuffed) breast of veal

  katenspek: hot smoked belly

  kalfstong: calf's tongue

  lever: cooked liver, usually larded

  ontbijtspek: cold smoked and rolled pork belly

  ossentong: ox-tongue

  paardenrookvlees: smoked, salted and dried horse meat

  pastrami: smoked, spiced lean meat, like *pekelvlees**

  pekel(vlees): cured beef (usually brisket), corned beef

  procureursspek: bacon; Dutch variety of pancetta

  rauwe ham: cured raw leg of pork

  rollade: rolled meat

  schouderham: boiled pork shoulder, deboned and amalgamated

  rookvlees: smoked, salted, dried beef

  ros(bief): roast beef

  spek: belly, back, bacon

  vetspek: fat back

  Zeeuws spek: salted, spicy marinated cooked pork belly

  zuurkoolspek: salted pork belly

vlokken: flakes

vol: full, complete

vossenbes: continental European cranberry, smaller than the American

vrucht: fruit

walnoot: walnut

warme bakker: bakery with oven

watergruwel: water gruel

waterkers: water cress 29, 40, 59

watermeloen: water melon 29, 40

Weesper mop: cookie made from almond paste 5

witbier: slightly sweet, wheaten (white) beer, excellent with spicy food (better than *pils**)

worst: sausage 22, 54, 59

   Amsterdamse leverworst: larded liver sausage

   Bifi: small cocktail salami, *bierworstje**

   bierworstje: small salami, eaten as finger food

   bloedworst: blood sausage, black pudding

   bakbloedworst: large, larded blood sausage, sliced and fried

   boterhamworst: luncheon meat, Dutch baloney

   braadworst: fresh sausage, to be fried

   Brabantse metworst: raw, smoked sausage, spreadable, like *theeworst**

   cervelaat: Dutch salami with pork and beef

   cocktailworst: mini-sausage (usually Frankfurter type)

   boerenmetworst: smoked dried sausage

   Gelderse: trad.: from Gelderland, the best pork. Now meaningless

   grillworst: grilled sausage

   Groninger leverworst: liver sausage, with extra cloves

   Groninger metworst: dried sausage, usually with extra cloves

   Haagse leverworst: common smooth liverwurst, to be sliced

   hausmacher: very coarse liverwurst with pieces meat and liver

   knakworst: Frankfurter type sausage, hot dog sausage

   knoflookworst: garlic sausage

   leverworst: liver sausage

   likkepot: liver sausage mixed with herbs etc.

   lunchworst: luncheon meat

   ossenworst: raw sausage made with seasoned beef – the best is smoked

palingworst: boiled sausage with pork and beef

rookworst: smoked boiled sausage, pork, sometimes beef or veal

Saksische leverworst: smooth, spreadable liver sausage

saucijsjes: fresh pork sausages, to be fried or grilled

Smac: Spam

smeerworst: any spreadable liver sausage

sterf–op–straat–worst: (litt: die in the street sausage) = *cervelaatworst**

theeworst: smoked spreadable fine sausage

tongenworst: boiled sausage with tongue

verse worst: fresh sausage

worstenbroodje: roll with sausage baked inside

Zaanse kermis: biscuit with coconut topping 59

zacht: soft

zakje, papieren/plastic: paper/plastic bag

zeevruchten: 1. seafood, seashells 2. chocolates in the shape of seashells

zoethout: liquorice/licorice stick 56

zoetjes: artificial sweeteners 25, 59

zoetstof: sweetener

zoute vlinder: palmier, savoury puff pastry cookie 5, 22

zoutjes: salty cookies 5, 59

zuidvruchten: mixed dried fruit 43, 59

zure bom: large sweet and sour gherkin 30

zure haring: herring filets pickled in spices and vinegar 30, 64

zure room: sour cream 59

zure zult: spicy terrine of brawn, shoulder and neck 22, 54

zuurstok: striped candy stick 34, 56

zwarte peper: black pepper 59

zwoerdmaag: (also pungel or katte) pig's stomach filled with heart and sausage meat, cooked and pickled 22, 54

PLACES TO GO

1. **Afhaal**: takeaway
2. **Albert Heijn**: largest supermarket chain
3. **Automatiek**: an automat with various snacks, usually hot, often part of a snackbar. Also called 'de muur' (the wall)
4. **Backerij** (a bakery with an attitude)
5. **Bakkerij**: bakery
6. **Banketbakkerij**: fine bakery, pâtisserie
7. **Bezorgzaak**: order and they deliver, caterer
8. **Boerenmarkt**: farmer's (organic) market
9. **Brasserie**: large café with extended snacks or dishes
10. **Broodbakkerij**: bread bakery
11. **Broodjeswinkel/broodjeszaak**: sandwichshop for filled rolls and alcoholfree drinks
12. **Broodtiek** (another bakery with an attitude)
13. **Café**: for drinks of all kinds (except cocktails) and small snacks; open till late at night
14. **Cafetaria**: fastfood restaurant
15. **Cafeteria**: selfservice fastfood restaurant, usually confused with cafetaria
16. **Cateraar**: caterer who serves parties
17. **Chocolaterie**: chocolate and sweets shop
18. **Coffeeshop**: for coffee, tea and soft drugs
19. **Comestibleszaak**: delicatessenshop, no eating, sometimes takeaway
20. **Confiserie**: almost identical with chocolaterie
21. **Croissanterie**: upmarket bakery, viennoiserie, also serving as broodjeswinkel
22. **Delicatessenwinkel**: grocery with specialized items and imported products
23. **Dimsumbar**
24. **Drankenhandel**: beer, wine and liquorshop (= *slijterij*)
25. **Drogist**: drugstore

26. **Espressobar**: just coffee, tea and sympathy, no drugs!
27. **Grand café**: like brasserie, large café with snacks and dishes
28. **Grillroom**: small restaurant specialized in grilled meats
29. **Groenteboer**: greengrocer, sometimes sells complete dishes and salads
30. **Haringkraam**: herringstall, sells just herring and some other fishy snacks
31. **HEMA**: department store
32. **IJssalon**: ice cream parlour
33. **Kaashandel/kaaswinkel**: cheese shop, sometimes sells filled rolls
34. **Kermis**: fair
35. **Koffiehuis**: coffeehouse, combining cheap coffee and simple sandwiches
36. **Koffieshop**: coffeeshop, for coffee, tea and soft drugs
37. **Koffiewinkel**: sells coffee beans, tealeaves and -bags and parafernalia for connoisseurs
38. **Kruidenier**: grocer, usually a supermarket, sells anything edible
39. **Lunchroom**: a sandwichshop with an extended assortment of dishes
40. **Markt**: the market, where anything goes
41. **Nachtcafé**: café open till 2 or 3 (weekends) at night (the law is about to be changed!)
42. **Natuurwinkel**: organic shop
43. **Notenbar**: nutshop
44. **Oliebollenkraam**: stall where *oliebollen** and *appelflappen** are fried and sold
45. **Petit restaurant**: small restaurant with simple dishes
46. **Pizzeria**: the same thing
47. **Poelier**: game and fowl is sold here
48. **Poffertjeskraam**: usually a baroque, mirrored tent where they serve *poffertjes** and pancakes
49. **Reformwinkel**: usually an alternative grocer with organic products
50. **Restaurant**
51. **Sandwichshop**: filled rolls, coffee and non-alcoholic drinks, matballs, croquettes

52. **Shoarmazaak**: Middle Eastern type snackbar with grilled meat and pitta bread
53. **Sigarenzaak**: tobacconist
54. **Slagerij**: butcher, sometimes complete dishes and filled rolls
55. **Snackbar**: usually deep fried factory made snacks, ice and soft drinks
56. **Snoepwinkel**: confiserie, sweets, candy
57. **Soepkeuken**: soupkitchens, new chains of usually freshly made, sometimes organic soups
58. **Steakhouse**: large grillroom
59. **Supermarkt**
60. **Sushibar**
61. **Tabakswinkel**: tobacconist
62. **Tearoom**: usually part of a fine bakery, serving tea and cakes
63. **Traiteur/traiterie**: takeaway
64. **Viswinkel**: fishmonger
65. **Vlaaiwinkel**: pie shop
66. **Warme bakker**: a baker who bakes his own bread
67. **Wijnhandel**: wine and liquor shop

WEIGHTS AND MEASURES

gram (1 g)
ons (100 g)
pond (500 g)
kilo (1000 g)

milliliter (1 ml)
centiliter (1 cl = 10 ml)
deciliter (1 dl = 100 ml)
liter (1 l = 1000 ml)

millimeter (1 mm)
centimeter (1 cm = 10 mm)
decimeter (1 dm = 100 mm)
meter (1 m = 1000 mm)
1 inch = 2,54 cm
1 foot = 30 cm
1 yard = 91 cm
1 stick of butter = 114 g

$32\ ^{\circ}F = 0\ ^{\circ}C$
$50\ ^{\circ}F = 10\ ^{\circ}C$
$100\ ^{\circ}F = 37\ ^{\circ}C$
$212\ ^{\circ}F = 100\ ^{\circ}C$
$(^{\circ}F - 32) \times 0,56 = ^{\circ}C$
$(1,8 \times ^{\circ}C) + 32 = ^{\circ}F$

BEST SHOPS

BREAD, PASTRY AND CONFECTIONERY

Annee
ORGANIC BREAD AND
PASTRY

RUNSTRAAT 25
1016 GJ, 623 53 22
BELLAMYSTRAAT 2
1053 BL, 618 31 13

MON-FRI 8.45 AM-6 PM,
SAT 9 AM-5 PM MON-FRI
8-17, SAT 8 AM-4 PM,
CLOSED TUE

The Australian
ICE-CREAM AND SWEETS
WWW.AUSTRALIANHOME
MADE.COM

LEIDSESTRAAT 101
1017 NZ, 622 08 97
SPUI 5
1012 WX, 627 44 30
HEILIGEWEG/SINGEL 437
1012 WP, 428 75 33
ARENA BOULEVARD 40
1101 DJ, 409 50 50

ALL CHAIN STORES:
DURING SUMMER 10 AM-
8 PM, DURING WINTER
10 AM-6 PM

Bakken met Passie
OLD-FASHIONED *VLOER-
BROOD, VIENNOISERIE*
AND PASTRY

ALBERT CUYP-
STRAAT 51-53
1072 CM, 670 13 76

TUE-SAT 8 AM-6 PM

171 **De Bakkerswinkel**
WWW.
172 DEBAKKERSWINKEL.NL

173

ROELOF HARTSTRAAT 68
1071 VM, 662 35 94
WARMOESSTRAAT 69
1012 HX, 489 80 00
FAX 489 78 78
REGULATEURSHUIS
WESTERPARK (FACING
'STADSDEELKANTOOR')

TUE-FRI 7 AM-6 PM, SAT 7
AM-5 PM, SUN 10 AM-4 PM
TUE-FRI 8 AM-6 PM, SAT 8
AM-5 PM, SUN 10 AM-5 PM

TUE-FRI 8 AM-6 PM, SAT 8
AM-5 PM, SUN 10 AM-5 PM

Beune
BOSSCHE BOL, PASTRY,
PAINTED CAKES BY
ORDER

HAARLEMMERDIJK 156
1013 JJ, 624 83 56

MON-FRI 8.30 AM-6 PM,
SAT 8 AM-5 PM

Arnold Cornelis

VAN BAERLESTRAAT 93
1071 AT, 662 12 28
ELANDSGRACHT 78
1016 TZ, 625 85 85
1E C. HUYGENSSTRAAT 78
1054 BX, 618 36 88

MON-FRI 8.30 AM-6 PM,
SAT 8.30 AM-5 PM

Crust and Crumbs
BREAD

HAARLEMMERSTRAAT 108
1013 EW, 528 64 30

MON 11 AM-6.30 PM,
TUE-FRI 8.30 AM-6.30 PM,
SAT 9 AM-5 PM

Délifrance
FRENCH BREAD

DAMRAK 83
1012 LN, 622 28 84

DAILY 8 AM-9 PM

Gary's Muffins
BAGELS

KINKERSTRAAT 140
1053 DZ, 412 30 25

MON-FRI 8.30 AM-6 PM,
SAT 9 AM-6 PM, SUN 10
AM-6 PM

Hartog
WHOLEMEAL BREAD,
AMANDELSPECULAAS

RUYSCHSTRAAT 56
1091 CE, 665 12 95

MON-FRI 7 AM-6 PM, SAT
6.30 AM-4.30 PM

Hendrikse
PASTRY, SWEETS

OVERTOOM 472
1054 JX, 618 04 72
TUSSEN MEER 75,
1068 EZ, 667 44 95

MON-FRI 8.30 AM-5.30 PM,
SAT 8.30 AM-4.30 PM
MON-FRI 8.30 AM-5.30 PM,
SAT 8.30 AM-5 PM

Holtkamp
PASTRY, CROQUETTES
WWW.BANKETBAKKERIJ
HOLTKAMP.NL

VIJZELGRACHT 15
1017 HM, 624 87 57

MON-FRI 8.30 AM-6 PM,
SAT UNTIL 5 PM

193 **Kismet**
TURKISH PASTRY
TAKEAWAY MEALS,
ALSO PARTY-CATERING

ALBERT CUYPSTRAAT 64
1072 CW, 671 47 68

DAILY 8 AM-10 PM

Kwekkeboom
BREAD AND PASTRY,
APPLEPIE, *OLIEBOLLEN*,
SAUCIJZENBROODJES
WWW.KWEKKEBOOM
BANKET.NL

REGULIERSBREE-
STRAAT 36
1017 CN, 623 12 05
LINNAEUSSTRAAT 80-86
1092 CN, 665 04 43

FERDINAND BOL-
STRAAT 119
1072 LG, 673 71 14

MON-FRI 9 AM-5.45 PM
SAT 9 AM-5.30 PM, SUN 12
NOON-6 PM
MON-FRI 8.30 AM-5.30 PM
SAT 9 AM-5 PM, CLOSED
SUN
MON-FRI 9 AM-5.45 PM
SAT 9 AM-5 PM, CLOSED
SUN

Lanskroon
PASTRY, APPLEPIE,
*GEVULDE KOEK, OLIEBOL-
LEN* SAUSAGE-ROLL

SINGEL 385
1012 WL, 623 77 43

TUE-FRI 8 AM-5.30 PM
SAT 9 AM-6 PM, SUN 10
AM-6 PM

Limmen
*BOTERKOEK, AMANDEL-
SPECULAAS*

ADM. DE RUIJTERWEG 79
1057 JZ, 618 29 26

MON-SAT 8 AM-5 PM

Mediterranée
MOROCCAN/FRENCH
BREAD, PASTRY, CROIS-
SANTS

HAARLEMMERDIJK 184
1013 JK, 620 35 50

MON-SAT 8 AM-7.30 PM,
SUN 8 AM-6 PM

Nur
TURKISH PASTRY

MOLUKKENSTRAAT 115
1095 BA, 665 59 82

MON-SAT 7 AM-9 PM, SUN
9 AM-8 PM

Outmayer
OLIEBOLLEN

I.A. REGULIERSBREE-
STRAAT 24
1017 CN, 624 14 96

DAILY 8.30 AM-8 PM

197 **Pompadour**
SWEETS, PASTRY,
APPLEPIE, CROISSANTS
WWW.PATISSERIE
POMPADOUR.COM

HUIDENSTRAAT 12
1016 ES, 623 95 54
KERKSTRAAT 148
1017 GR, 330 09 81

MON-FRI 9 AM-6 PM, SAT
8.30 AM-5 PM
MON-SAT 10 AM-5 PM,
CLOSED SUN

Runneboom
ALLINSONBROOD,
FRENCH BREAD

1E VAN DER HELST-
STRAAT 49
1073 AD, 673 59 41

MON/WED/FRI 7 AM-5 PM
TUE/THU/SAT 7 AM-4 PM

Rijkhoff
*BOTERKOEK, GEVULDE
SPECULAAS*

BOS & LOMMERWEG 319
1055 DZ, 684 64 57

MON-SAT 7 AM-5 PM

Saray
BALKAN,
PASTRY-SPECIALTIES

JAVASTRAAT 121
1094 HD, 665 06 72

MON-SAT 9 AM-5 PM

De taart van m'n tante
'EMOTIONAL PASTRY',
BY ORDER
WWW.DETAART.COM

FERDINAND BOLSTRAAT 10
1072 LJ, 776 46 00
FAX 776 46 04

DAILY 10 AM-6 PM

Theeboom
BREAD AND PASTRY ON
SUNDAYS
WWW.THEEBOOM.NL

MAASSTRAAT 16
1078 HJ, 662 48 27
BOLESTEIN 45-47
1081 CR, 642 70 03

8.30 AM-5 PM,
CLOSED MON, TUE & SAT
8.30 AM-5 PM,
CLOSED TUE & SAT

Unlimited Delicious
BONBON-WORKSHOP

HAARLEMMERSTRAAT 122
1013 EX, 622 48 29

MON-SAT 9 AM-6 PM,
CLOSED SUN

CATERERS

0039
ITALIAN

TWEEDE TUINDWARS-
STRAAT 14
1015 RZ, 421 05 67

DAILY 11 AM-9 PM,
CLOSED SUN

Bombachas do Brasil
BRAZILIAN
WWW.BOMBACHAS.NL

KINKERSTRAAT 338
1053 GE, 616 21 30

SUN-FRI 10 AM-9 PM

92 **Bos**
CATERING
WWW.VANDEMARKT.NL

SCHOLLENBRUGSTRAAT 9
1091 EZ, 692 89 05

Il Commendatore
ITALIAN CATERING
WWW.COMMENDATORE.NL

VENETIËHOF 21
1019 NA, 419 43 64
FAX 419 57 06

Cucina Casalinga
ITALIAN
WWW.CASALINGA.NL.

STADIONWEG 271
1076 NZ, 679 15 92

TUE-FRI 11 AM-8 PM, SAT
11 AM-6 PM

181 **Le Delizie**
ITALIAN
WWW.LEDELIZIE.NL

VIJZELGRACHT 17
1017 HM, 622 68 71

MON-SAT 10 AM-11 PM,
SUN 11 AM-11 PM

Gaffaf mediterrane
KURDISH & GREEK
CATERING AND
DELICATESSEN

1E CONST. HUYGENS-
STRAAT 41
1054 BR, T / F 618 44 52

MON-FRI 9 AM-7 PM, SAT
9 AM-6 PM

**Grekas Griekse
Traiterie**

SINGEL 311
1012 WJ, 620 35 90

WED-SUN 5-10 PM

Indian Express
INDIAN
WWW.INDIANEXPRESS.NL

PIETER LANGENDIJK-
STRAAT 37
1054 XX, 612 84 88

DAILY 4.30-10.30 PM

193 **Kismet**
TURKISH PASTRY
TAKEAWAY MEALS,
ALSO PARTY-CATERING

ALBERT CUYPSTRAAT 64
1072 CW, 671 47 68

MON-SUN 8 AM- 9 PM

Lezzet
TURKISH

HOOFDDORPWEG 15
1059 CS, 615 05 84

DAILY 9 AM-9 PM

199 **Sal Meijer**
KOSHER SANDWICHSHOP

SCHELDESTRAAT 45
1078 GG, 673 13 13

SUN-THU 9.30 AM-7.30 PM,
FRI 9.30 AM-2 PM

No Sushi
JAPANESE/SUSHI
WWW.NOSUSHI.NL

VAN BAERLESTRAAT 87
1071 AT, 672 12 34 OR
0900 667 87 44

MON-SAT 11 AM-9 PM,
SUN 2-8 PM

Nonna Papera
ITALIAN

SCHELDESTRAAT 63
1078 GH, 662 69 53

MON-SAT 10 AM-7.30 PM,
CLOSED SUN

Pasteuning
WINE AND CATERING

WILLEMSPARKWEG 11
1071 GN, 662 00 23

MON-SAT 7.30 AM-6 PM,
TUE 7.30 AM-1 PM

Peper en Zuur
SURINAMESE

HEISTEEG 5
1012 WC, T/F 420 40 98

MON-SAT 11 AM-8 PM, THU
UNTIL 9.30 PM, CLOSED
SUN

Raïnaraï
NORTH-AFRICAN,
MEDITERRANEAN
WWW.RAINARAI.NL

PRINSENGRACHT 252
1016 HG, 624 97 91

TUE-SUN 12 NOON-10 PM

Ralph's Asian Wonderfood ASIAN	1E VAN DER HELST-STRAAT 37 1073 AC, 670 90 07	MON-WED 12 NOON-9 PM, THU-SAT 12 NOON-10 PM, SUN 4-9 PM
Renzo's delicatessen	VAN BAERLESTRAAT 67 1071 AR, 673 16 73	MON-FRI 10 AM-9 PM, SAT & SUN 11 AM-7 PM
Tom Yam Thai	UTRECHTSESTRAAT 55 1017 VJ, 623 15 64	DAILY 4-9 PM
La Romanca Mea ROMANIAN WWW.LAROMANCAMEA.NL	JAN PIETER HEYE-STRAAT 115 1054 MD, 619 90 53	MON-FRI 11 AM-9.30 PM, SAT 11 AM-8 PM, SUN 3-8 PM
Roos en Noor INTERNATIONAL WWW.ROOSENNOOR.NL	BARON TINDALSTRAAT 148 1019 TX, 419 14 40	DAILY 12 NOON-9 PM
Eetwinkel Zwaan FRENCH WWW. EETWINKEL ZWAAN.NL	ZUIDPLEIN 22 (NEAR WTC) 1077 XV, 442 21 12	MON-FRI 12 NOON-8 PM

CHEESE

Arxhoek	DAMSTRAAT 19 1012 JL, 622 91 18	MON-FRI 9 AM-6 PM, SAT 9 AM-5 PM, SUN 11 AM-4 PM
Erik's delicatessen CHEESE, WINE, OIL, ETC. WWW.ERIKS DELICATESSEN.NL	BEUKENPLEIN 16 1091 KH, 694 30 77	MON-FRI 8 AM-6 PM, SAT 9 AM-5 PM
De Kaaskamer	RUNSTRAAT 7 1016 GJ, 623 34 83	MON 12 NOON-6 PM, TUE-FRI 9 AM-6 PM, SAT 9 AM-5 PM, SUN 12 NOON-5 PM
192 **Kef, De Franse Kaasmakers** WWW.KAASVANKEF.NL	MARNIXSTRAAT 192 1016 TJ, 420 00 97	WED/THU/FRI 12 NOON-8 PM, SAT 10 AM-6 PM, SUN 12 NOON-6 PM
Market on Albert Cuypstraat		MON-SAT

CIGARS

John N. Andringa	REGULIERSBREESTRAAT 2 1017 CN, 623 28 36	MON-SAT 9 AM-6 PM, SUN 12 NOON-5 PM
Hajenius WWW.HAJENIUS.COM	ROKIN 92-96 1012 KZ, 623 74 94	MON 12 NOON-6 PM, TUE-SAT 9.30 AM-6 PM, SUN 12 NOON-5 PM

COFFEE, TEA AND SPICES

Brandmeester's Coffee ESPRESSO, BEANS	VAN BAERLESTRAAT 13 1071 AM, 675 78 88	MON-FRI 9 AM-6 PM, SAT 9 AM-5.30 PM SUN 12 NOON-5 PM
	ARENA BOULEVARD 160 1101 DJ, 567 52 52	MON-FRI 10 AM-6 PM, THU 10 AM-9 PM, SAT 10 AM-5.30 PM 1ST SUNDAY OF THE MONTH 11 AM-5 PM
Coffee Company WWW.COFFEECOMPANY.NL ESPRESSO, BEANS	KALVERTOREN 1012 WP, 422 94 23 BEETHOVENSTRAAT 43 1077 HN, 672 1258 LEIDSESTRAAT 60 1017 PC, 428 22 41 HAARLEMMERDIJK 62 1013 JE, 626 37 76 1E VAN DER HELST- STRAAT 62 B 1072 NX, 673 17 69 MIDDENWEG 32 1097 BP, 468 96 82 FERDINAND BOL- STRAAT 38 1072 LK, 573 00 00 KINKERSTRAAT 332 A 1053 GD, 489 84 00 NIEUWE DOELENSTRAAT 24 1012 CP, 420 7364	VARIOUS OPENING HOURS, CHECK WEBSITE
Jacob Hooy & Co	KLOVENIERSBURG- WAL 10-12 1012 CT, 624 30 41	MON/TUE/WED/FRI 10 AM- 6 PM, THU 10 AM-9 PM, SAT 10 AM-5 PM
Simon Lévelt COFFEE AND TEA	FERDINAND BOL- STRAAT 154 1072 LS, 400 40 60 STATIONSPLEIN 14 (IN CENTRAL STATION) 1012 AB, 428 58 87 PRINSENGRACHT 180 1016 HB, 624 08 23 KINKERSTRAAT 109 1053 DK, 489 59 65	MON 12 NOON-6 PM, TUE-FRI 10 AM-6 PM, SAT 10 AM-5 PM MON-FRI 8 AM-8 PM, SAT 9 AM-8 PM, SUN 12 NOON-7 PM MON-FRI 10 AM-6 PM, SAT 9 AM-5 PM MON 12 NOON-6 PM, TUE-FRI 10 AM-6 PM, SAT 10 AM-5 PM

DELICATESSEN, PROVISIONS, *PRIMEURS*

Asian, Surinamese

Meidi-Ya JAPANESE	BEETHOVENSTRAAT 18-20 1077 JG, 673 74 10	MON-FRI 10.30 AM-6 PM, SAT 9 AM-5 PM
Thai Shop THAI	KONINGSSTRAAT 42 1011 EW, 620 99 00	MON-SAT 10 AM-6 PM, SUN 11 AM-5 PM
[208] **Tjin's International Foodstore**	EERSTE VAN DER HELST- STRAAT 64 1072 NZ, 671 77 08	MON-SAT 9.30 AM-8 PM
Toko Dun Yong CHINESE WWW.DUNYONG.COM	STORMSTEEG 9/ ZEEDIJK 83 1012 BD, 622 17 63	MON-SAT 9 AM-6 PM, SUN 12 NOON-6 PM

Toko Ramée
INDONESIAN

FERDINAND BOL-
STRAAT 74
1072 LM, 662 20 25

TUE-FRI 10 AM-7 PM,
SAT 10 AM-6 PM

Wah Nam Hong
ASIAN

GELDERSEKADE 90-92
1012 BM, 627 03 03

MON-FRI 9 AM-6 PM,
SAT UNTIL 5.30 PM

International

Caulils
WWW.CAULILS.COM

HAARLEMMERSTRAAT 115
1013 EM, 412 00 27
FAX 412 53 47

MON-FRI 12 NOON-8 PM,
SAT 10 AM-6 PM,
SUN 12 NOON-6 PM

Eichholtz
BAGELS

LEIDSESTRAAT 48
1017 PC, 622 03 05

MON 10 AM-6.30 PM,
TUE/WED/FRI/SAT
9 AM-6.30 PM
THU 9 AM-9 PM,
SUN 12 NOON-6.30 PM

Erik's delicatessen
WWW.ERIKS
DELICATESSEN.NL

BEUKENPLEIN 16
1091 KH, 694 30 77

MON-FRI 8 AM-6 PM,
SAT UNTIL 5 PM

Loekie
CRABSALAD

PRINSENGRACHT 705-A
1017 JV, 624 42 30
FAX 625 22 37
UTRECHTSESTRAAT 57
1017 VJ, 624 37 40
FAX 620 68 85

MON-SAT 9 AM-5 PM,
SUN 11 AM-5 PM

MON-FRI 9 AM-6 PM,
WED 9 AM-1 PM,
SAT 9 AM-5 PM

Oceaan

C. VAN EESTEREN-
LAAN 21-22
1019 JK, 419 75 51
FAX 419 75 52

MON-FRI 12 NOON-9 PM,
SAT 11 AM-9 PM,
SUN 12 NOON-9 PM

26 **Puyck**
WWW.PUYCK.NL

SARPHATIPARK 34
1072 PB, 675 16 86
FAX 672 01 39

THU-FRI 12 NOON-9 PM,
SAT 11 AM-6 PM

Italian

81 **Le Delizie**
WWW.LEDELIZIE.NL

VIJZELGRACHT 17
1017 HM, 622 68 71

MON-SAT 10 AM-11 PM,
SUN 11 AM-11 PM

Isole
I.A. SICILY, SARDINIA

LINDENSTRAAT 48
1015 KX, 421 13 42

WED-FRI 12 NOON-6 PM,
SAT 10 AM-5 PM

Pasta Di Mamma

P.C. HOOFTSTRAAT 52
1071 CA, 664 83 14

MON-SAT 9 AM-7 PM,
SUN 12 NOON-7 PM

Uliveto
MEDITERRANEAN
PRODUCTS

WETERINGSCHANS 118
1017 XT, 423 00 99

MON-FRI 11 AM-8 PM,
SAT 12 NOON-6 PM

Middle East

Perzisch Huis

ROZENGRACHT 56
1016 DN, 423 21 04

DAILY 10 AM-10 PM

Super Roos

ROZENGRACHT 135
1016 LV, 639 39 04

DAILY 10.30 AM-10 PM

De Volkskruidentuin
SPICES & DRIED FOOD

KINKERSTRAAT 142
1053 EG, 06 1061 11 09

MON-SAT 9 AM-6 PM

Scottish

Stelle Robertson
SCOTTISH PASTRY,
BREAD, FINE JAMS AND
MARMELADES
WWW.STELLEROBERTSON.NL

AT THE FARMERS' MARKET,
NOORDERMARKT, SATUR-
DAY

Southern European

Casa Bocage
PORTUGUESE
DELICATESSEN

HAARLEMMER-
STRAAT 111 A
1013 EM, 427 45 55
FAX 427 59 39

MON 1-8 PM, TUE-FRI 12
NOON-8 PM, SAT 10 AM-7
PM, SUN 12 NOON-5 PM

Casa del Gusto
UMBRIA & TUSCANY

KERKSTRAAT 121
1017 GE, 330 8330

TUE/THU/FRI/SAT 11 AM-8
PM, WED 3-8 PM, SUN 12
NOON-6 PM

Casa Molero
SPANISH & PORTUGUESE

GERARD DOUSTRAAT 66
1072 VV, 676 17 07

WED-FRI 10 AM-6 PM,
SAT 9 AM-5 PM

Hollandaluz
ANDALUCIA & SPAIN
WWW.HOLLANDALUZ.NL

HAARLEMMERSTRAAT 71
1013 EL, T / F 330 28 88

MON-FRI 10.30 AM-
6.30 PM,
SAT 10.30 AM-5.30 PM

Mouwes
KOSHER DELICATESSEN

KASTELENSTRAAT 261
1082 EG, 661 01 80

MON-THU 9 AM-5 PM,
FRI 8 AM-2 PM,
SUN 10 AM-5 PM

Oil, vinegar, etc.

Meeuwig en Zn.

HAARLEMMERSTRAAT 70
1013 ET, 626 52 86

MON-FRI 11 AM-6.30 PM,
SAT 10 AM-5.30 PM

Olivaria

HAZENSTRAAT 2 A
1016 SP, 638 35 52

MON 2-6 PM, TUE-SAT 11
AM-6 PM

Organic food

De Aanzet

FRANS HALSSTRAAT 27
1072 BK, 673 34 15

MON-FRI 9 AM-6 PM, SAT
9 AM-5 PM

De Belly

NIEUWE LELIESTRAAT 174
1015 HG, 330 94 83

MON-FRI 8.30 AM-6.30 PM,
SAT UNTIL 5.30 PM

Delicious Food

WESTERSTRAAT 24
1015 MJ, 320 30 70
FAX 320 20 41

MON-FRI 10 AM-7 PM,
SAT 10 AM-6 PM, SUN 11
AM-3 PM, CLOSED TUE

**Natuurwinkel
Weteringschans**

WETERINGSCHANS 133
1017 SC, 638 40 83

MON-SAT 8 AM-8 PM,
SUN 11 AM-7 PM

De Natuurwinkel

AALSMEERWEG 8
1E CONST. HUYGENS-
STRAAT 49
ELANDSGRACHT 118
HAARLEMMERDIJK 174
MARATHONWEG 21-23
SCHELDESTRAAT 53
1E VAN SWINDENSTRAAT 30
VAN WOUSTRAAT 86

VARIOUS OPENING
HOURS, CHECK: WWW.
DENATUURWINKEL.COM

De Weegschaal

JODENBREESTRAAT 20
1011 NK, 624 17 65

MON-FRI 9 AM-6 PM,
SAT 9 AM-5 PM

FISH

Altena
HERRING

BOOTH RIJKSMUSEUM/
STADHOUDERSKADE

De Boer
HERRING

BOOTH FACING OSDORP-
PLEIN 624

Fishes
WEBSITE WWW.FISHES.NL

UTRECHTSESTRAAT 98
1017 VS, 626 85 00
JOH. VERHULSTSTRAAT 110
1071 NL, 672 43 34

MON-FRI 10 AM-6:30 PM,
SAT 9 AM-5 PM
MON-FRI 10 AM-7 PM,
SAT 9 AM-5 PM

**Frank's Smoke
House**
SMOKED FISH, MEAT,
CHEESE, ETC
WWW.SMOKEHOUSE.NL

WITTENBURGER-
GRACHT 303
1018 ZL, 670 0774

TUE-FRI 9 AM-6 PM,
SAT 9 AM-5 PM

Jan Hendriks
SPECIALTY: FISHCAKES

HAGELAND 111
(NIEUW-SLOTEN)
1066 SB, 669 68 15

MON-FRI 8 AM-6 PM,
SAT 8 AM-4 PM

Kromhout
HERRING

BOOTH SINGEL/RAADHUIS-
STRAAT

Meer dan Vis

2E EGELANTIERSDWARS-
STRAAT 13
1015 SB, 422 30 30

TUE-FRI 10.30 AM-7 PM,
SAT 9 AM-6 PM, SUN 12
NOON-6 PM, CLOSED MON

Kees Tol
HERRING

BOOTH AT THE END OF
OVERTOOM
683 02 08,

TUE-FRI 9.30 AM-6 PM,
SAT 9.30 AM-5 PM

FRENCH FRIES / CHIPS

Holland-België

ROETERSSTRAAT 2 A
1018 WC, 622 97 77

MON-SAT 4 PM-1 AM,
SUN 2 PM-1 AM

Vlaams Friteshuis

VOETBOOGSTEEG 33
1012 XK, 624 60 75

TUE-SAT 11 AM-6 PM,
SUN & MON 12 NOON-6 PM

**Wil Graanstra's
Frites**
SINCE 1956

BOOTH WESTERMARKT

TUE-SAT 11 AM-6 PM

ICE-CREAM

The Australian
WWW.AUSTRALIAN
HOMEMADE.COM

LEIDSESTRAAT 101
1017 NZ, 622 08 97
SPUI 5
1012 WX, 627 44 30
HEILIGEWEG/SINGEL 437
1012 WP, 428 75 33
ARENA BOULEVARD 40
1101 DJ, 409 50 50

ALL CHAIN STORES:
DURING SUMMER:10 AM-
8 PM, DURING WINTER:
10 AM-6 PM

Peppino IJssalon

1E SWEELINCKSTRAAT 16
1073 CM, 676 49 10

DAILY 11 AM-11 PM
CLOSED OCTOBER UNTIL
APRIL

Pisa

SCHELDEPLEIN 10
1078 GR, 671 55 77

DAILY 12 NOON-MIDNIGHT
CLOSED OCTOBER UNTIL
HALF APRIL

MARKETS

At Albert Cuypstraat		MON-SAT
At Dapperstraat		MON-SAT
At Ten Katestraat		MON-SAT
At Lindengracht		SAT
Farmers' market	AT NIEUWMARKT	SAT
	AT NOORDERMARKT	SAT
Caribbean market	AT GANZENHOEF	WED & SAT
	AT AMSTERDAMSE POORT	MON & THU
	KRAAIENNEST	TUE & FRI

MEAT

Siem van der Gragt ORGANIC MEAT	ELANDSGRACHT 116 1016 VB, 623 43 87	MON-FRI 8 AM-6 PM, SAT UNTIL 5 PM
Hergo *AMSTERDAMSE LEVER- WORST, HAUSMACHER, ROOKWORST* (VEAL OR BEEF)	BEETHOVENSTRAAT 49 1077 HN, 671 30 98 MAASSTRAAT 53 BUITENVELDERTSE- LAAN 40 & 166 BINNENHOF 6 G, AMSTEL- VEEN	MON-FRI 8 AM-6 PM, SAT 7.30 AM-5 PM IDEM, SAT UNTIL 4 PM IDEM, SAT UNTIL 4 PM IDEM, SAT UNTIL 5 PM
Koopmans *AMSTERDAMSE LEVER- WORST*	ELANDSGRACHT 100 1016 VA, 623 84 80	MON/WED/THU/FRI 8.30 AM-6 PM, TUE 8.30 AM- 1 PM, SAT 7.30 AM-5 PM
De Leeuw, Fred en Yolanda WAGYU, TRUFFLES	UTRECHTSESTRAAT 92 1017 VS, 623 02 35	TUE-FRI 8 AM-6 PM, SAT 7 AM-5 PM
Marcus KOSHER, *OSSENWORST KALFSLEVERWORST, ROOKWORST* (VEAL OR BEEF),	WAALSTRAAT 17 1078 BP, 662 43 02	WED & THU 9 AM-5 PM, FRI 8.30 AM-1 PM
Pastijn *GELDERSE ROOKWORST*	HOGEWEG 1 B 1098 BT, 694 85 82	MON-FRI 8 AM-6 PM, SAT 8 AM-4 PM, CLOSED WED
D. Reinhart *GELDERSE ROOKWORST*	LIJNBAANSSTEEG 10 1012 TE, 623 03 66	MON-FRI 7.30 AM-6 PM, SAT 7 AM-5 PM
De Rooy *GELDERSE ROOKWORST*	HAARLEMMERSTRAAT 61 1013 EK, 624 49 05	MON-FRI 7.30 AM-6.30 PM, SAT 7.30 AM-5 PM
De Wit SAUSAGES, OWN CATTLE	WAKKERSTRAAT 13 1097 CB, 665 30 74	MON-FRI 8 AM-5.30 PM, SAT 8 AM-4 PM

VEGETABLES, FRUIT AND NUTS

Gotjé, de Nootzaak NUTS AND SUBTROPICAL FRUIT	MARKET IN DIEMEN MARKET ON LINDENGRACHT 06 55 700 700	WED SAT

Kamman Fruitprimeurs	BEETHOVENSTRAAT 50 1077 JK, 679 49 14	MON-FRI 9 AM-7 PM, SAT 8 AM-5 PM
Labes	KORTE PRINSENGRACHT 97 1013 GR, 624 32 75	MON-FRI 8 AM-6 PM, CLOSED WED, SAT 8 AM-5 PM
Morgan's groenten en fruit EXOTICS AND FIRSTLINGS	LINDENGRACHT 158 1015 KK, 620 24 57 SATURDAY ON THE MAR- KET FACING THE SHOP	TUE-FRI 8 AM-6 PM SATURDAY
Ron's groenten en fruit	HUIDENSTRAAT 26 1016 ET, 626 16 68	TUE-FRI 8 AM-6 PM, SAT 8 AM-5 PM

WINE, BEER, SPIRITS & OTHER DRINKS

De Bierkoning WWW.BIERKONING.NL	PALEISSTRAAT 125 1012 ZL, 625 23 36	MON 1-7 PM, TUE/WED/FRI 11 AM-7 PM, THU 11 AM-9 PM, SAT 11 AM-6 PM, SUN 1-5 PM
Chabrol WWW.CHABROLWINES.COM	HAARLEMMERSTRAAT 7 1013 EH, 622 27 81	MON-SAT 9 AM-7 PM, THU & FRI UNTIL 8 PM, SUN 12 NOON-6 PM
Elzinga Wijnen	FREDERIKSPLEIN 1 1017 XK, 623 72 70	MON & TUE 1-6 PM, WED-FRI 10 AM-6 PM, SAT 10 AM-5 PM
De Gouden Ton WWW.DEGOUDENTON.NL	WILLEMSPARKWEG 158 1071 HS, 679 62 31	MON 1-6 PM, TUE-FRI 10 AM-6 PM, SAT 10 AM-5 PM
Hart's Wijnhandel WWW.HARTSWIJN.NL	VIJZELGRACHT 27 1017 HN, 623 83 50	MON 1-6 PM, TUE-FRI 10 AM-6 PM, SAT 10 AM-5 PM
De Logie WWW.DELOGIE.NL	BEETHOVENSTRAAT 27 1077 HM, 662 62 08	MON 1-6 PM, TUE-FRI 9 AM-6 PM, SAT 10 AM-5 PM
Noord's Wijnhandel	SINGEL 516-518 1017 AX, 623 93 67	TUE-SAT NOON-6 PM
Otterman FRENCH WINES WWW.OTTERMAN.NL	KEIZERSGRACHT 300 1016 EW, 625 50 88 FAX 638 35 93	MON 1-6 PM, TUE-FRI 10.30 AM-6 PM, SAT 10.30 AM-5.30 PM
Quinta Wijnhandel & Wijntapperij PORTUGUESE WINES AND PORTS, ABSINTHE WWW.QUINTA-WIJNEN.NL	NIEUWE LELIESTRAAT 4 1015 SP, 427 02 26 FAX 618 33 36	MON-FRI 1.30-6.30 PM, SAT 10.30 AM-6.30 PM, SUN 1.30-5.30 PM
Renalda, De Wijnwinkel WWW.WIJNWINKEL.COM ITALIAN WINE	RUNSTRAAT 23 1016 GJ, 638 01 57 FAX 627 45 79	TUE-FRI 11 AM-6 PM, SAT UNTIL 5 PM
De Vreng en Zonen SPIRITS	NIEUWENDIJK 75 1012 MC, 624 45 81	MON-SAT 10 AM-6 PM

De Waterwinkel
WWW.DEWATERWINKEL.NL

ROELOF HARTSTRAAT 10
1071 VH, 675 59 32

MON 1-6 PM, TUE-FRI
10 AM-6 PM,
SAT 10 AM-5 PM

A. van Wees
WWW.DE-OOIEVAAR.NL

DRIEHOEKSTRAAT 10
1015 GL, 626 77 52

MON-FRI 9 AM-5 PM

**Wijnhandel Boelen
en Boelen**
WWW.WIJNBEURS
WINKEL.NL

RUSTENBURGERSTRAAT 387
1072 GV, 644 2474
FAX 613 50 64

MON 1-7 PM, TUE-FRI
10 AM-9 PM,
SAT 10 AM-6 PM

Wynand Fockink
WWW.WYNAND-FOCKINK.NL
VARIETY OF SPIRITS

PIJLSTEEG 31
1012 HH, 639 26 95

DAILY 3-9 PM

COOKING UTENSILS

Duikelman
WWW.DUIKELMAN.NL

FERDINAND BOL-
STRAAT 68
1072 LM, 671 22 30

TUE-FRI 9.30 AM-6 PM,
SAT 9.30 AM-5 PM

Studio Bazar
WWW.STUDIOBAZAR.COM

REGULIERSDWARS-
STRAAT 60-62
1017 BM, 622 08 30
KEIZERSGRACHT 709
1017 DW, 622 28 58
BEETHOVENSTRAAT 31
1077 HM, 471 44 47
WINKELCENTRUM
GELDERLANDPLEIN
W. VAN WELDAMMELAAN 27
1082 KT, 644 85 46

ALL CHAIN STORES:
MON-SAT 10 AM-6 PM,
FOR SHOPPINGNIGHTS
CHECK WEBSITE

Zwilling
J.A. HENCKELS
KNIVES
WWW.ZWILLING.COM

P.C. HOOFTSTRAAT 43
1071 BM, 671 42 20

MON 10 AM-6 PM,
TUE-FRI 9.30 AM-6 PM,
SAT 10 AM-5 PM,
1ST SUN OF THE MONTH
12 NOON-5 PM

COOKING COURSES AND BOOKS

**La Cuisine
Française**
WWW.
LACUISINEFRANCAISE.NL

HERENGRACHT 314
1016 CD, 627 87 25

Donna's Culitours
A CULINARY TOUR WITH
COOKING LESSON AND
MEAL
WWW.
DONNASCULITOURS.NL

364 11 93

**Internationale
Proeftafel**
WWW.PROEFTAFEL.COM

RUYSDAELSTRAAT 34-36
1071 XD, 400 45 64

BY APPOINTMENT

**Keizer Culinair
Kookschool**
COOKING LESSONS
WWW.KEIZERCULINAIR.NL

KEIZERSGRACHT 376
1016 GA, 427 92 76

Kinderkookkafé
COOKING LESSONS FOR
CHILDREN
WWW.KINDERKOOKKAFE.NL

VONDELPARK 6 B (KATTEN-
LAANTJE, EXIT OVERTOOM
325)
1071 AA, 625 32 57

KIDS 0-12 JR, DAILY
10 AM-8 PM

Kookboekhandel
BOOKSTORE SPECIALISED
IN CULINARY BOOKS
WWW.KOOKBOEKHAN-
DEL.COM

RUNSTRAAT 26
1016 GK, 622 47 68

MON 1-6 PM, TUE-FRI
11 AM-6 PM, THU 11 AM-
9 PM, SAT 11 AM-5 PM

**Kookstudio Dennis
Leeuw**
WWW.
KOOKSTUDIOLEEUW.COM

HAARLEMMER-
HOUTTUINEN 535
1013 GM, 620 40 70

Unlimited Delicious
BONBON-ATELIER
WWW.
UNLIMITEDDELICIOUS.NL

HAARLEMMERSTRAAT 122
1013 EX, 622 48 29

MON-SAT 9 AM-6 PM,
CLOSED SUN

Volksuniversiteit
WWW.VOLKSUNIVERSITEIT
AMSTERDAM.NL

RAPENBURGSTRAAT 73
1011 VK, 626 16 26

Like any city Amsterdam has a huge variety of restaurants, maybe because of the fact that Amsterdam has been an important international harbor. But its rich colonial past is another important factor.

There are posh, formal restaurants and informal, simple eateries.

Usually one looks for a place within a special category, so I grouped them according to cuisine. The extensive French cuisine, like anywhere else the most important restaurant style, I have divided in simple, average and top of the range.

Amsterdam counts over 2000 establishments, but *Delicious Amsterdam* presents only those restaurants that I wholeheartedly recommend, because I have personally visited and judged them. But even among the recommendable places there are good ones and better ones. As is customary in other guides, I have rewarded the best ones with a star system:

* = above average
** = very good
*** = excellent

The ones without an asterisk are still good restaurants.
The price you can expect is indicated with a

€ = cheap
€€ = average
€€€ = expensive

All other indications mentioned are self-evident.

For your convenience, a street plan has been added (see page 120-123).

As Amsterdam is relatively small, you should have no problems finding any place mentioned in *Delicious Amsterdam*.

BEST RESTAURANTS

AFRICAN — MIDDLE EAST

* De Aardige Pers

€ PERSIAN
1 TWEEDE HUGO DE GROOT-
STRAAT 13 B
1052 LA, OUD-WEST
T 400 31 07

OPEN DAILY 4 PM-
MIDNIGHT
TAKEAWAY POSSIBLE
UNTIL 10 PM
RESERVATION REC.
SEATING: 50
GROUPS: MAX. 50

CATERING
CASH PAYMENT ONLY
MUSIC: FOLKLORISTIC,
SOMETIMES LIVE MUSIC
AT WEEKENDS
AMBIENCE: SIMPLE,
FOLKLORISTIC

The way the Persians cook at home.

* Artist

€ LEBANESE
2 TWEEDE JAN STEEN-
STRAAT 1
1073 VK, OUD-ZUID
T 671 42 64

OPEN 5-11 PM,
CLOSED MON
RESERVATION REC.
SEATING: 50
GROUPS: MAX. 50
BAR
TERRACE

TAKEAWAY POSSIBLE
CATERING
MUSIC: JAZZ-FOLKLORIS-
TIC, SOMETIMES LIVE
AMBIENCE: ORIENTAL

The French cuisine of the Arab world by two elder Lebanese brothers.

Asmara

ERITREAN KITCHEN
€ JONAS DANIËL MEIJER-
3 PLEIN 8
1011 RH, CENTRUM
T 627 10 02

OPEN 5-10 PM,
CLOSED MON
RESERVATION REC.
SEATING: 50
GROUPS: MAX. 25
BAR
CASH PAYMENT ONLY

MUSIC: AFRICAN
AMBIENCE: SIMPLE,
FOLKLORISTIC

The simplest of the simple.

Bazar

€ MIDDLE EAST
4 ALBERT CUYPSTRAAT 182
1073 BL, OUD-ZUID
T 675 05 44 / F 673 21 96
WWW.
BAZARAMSTERDAM.NL

OPEN MON-THU 8 AM-11
PM, FRI 8 AM-MIDNIGHT,
SAT 9 AM-MIDNIGHT, SUN
9 AM-11 PM, DINNER
FROM 5 PM
RESERVATION REC.
SEATING: 240
GROUPS: MAX. 80

BAR
AIRCONDITIONING
TAKEAWAY POSSIBLE
MUSIC: WORLDMUSIC
AMBIENCE: ORIENTAL

Value for money in a huge bazar-like hall.

Beyrouth

€ LEBANESE
5 KINKERSTRAAT 18
1053 DV, OUD-WEST
T/F 616 06 35

OPEN DAILY 5-11 PM
RESERVATION REC.
SEATING: 50
GROUPS: MAX. 30
BAR
TAKEAWAY POSSIBLE

CATERING
NO CREDITCARDS
MUSIC: FOLKLORISTIC
AMBIENCE: ROMANTIC-
FOLKLORISTIC-INFORMAL

Refined meals, especially the meze tables.

* Eufraat

€ ASSYRIC
6 EERSTE VAN DER HELST-
STRAAT 72
1072 NZ, OUD-ZUID
T 672 05 79

OPEN 11 AM-10.30 PM,
SUN 5-10.30 PM,
CLOSED MON
RESERVATION REC. AT
WEEKENDS
SEATING: 42
GROUPS: MAX. 35

BAR
TERRACE
NO DOGS
TAKEAWAY POSSIBLE
MUSIC: FOLKLORISTIC
AMBIENCE: MODERN-
SIMPLE

Straightforward Middle Eastern food, homemade yoghurt etc.

* Kilimanjaro

€ **PAN-AFRICAN**
7 RAPENBURGERPLEIN 6
1011 VB, CENTRUM
T 622 34 85 / F 665 94 70

OPEN 5-10 PM,
CLOSED MON
RESERVATION REC.
SEATING: 22
GROUPS: MAX. 12
TERRACE

CATERING
CASH PAYMENT ONLY
MUSIC: FOLKLORISTIC
AMBIENCE: SIMPLE

Real Pan-African; try the special drinks!

* Klein Perzië

€ **MIDDLE EAST**
8 DE CLERCQSTRAAT 18
1052 ND, OUD-WEST
T 612 88 27
WWW.KLEINPERZIE.NL

OPEN DAILY 5-10 PM
RESERVATION REC.
SEATING: 45
GROUPS: MAX. 12
BAR
TERRACE
AIRCONDITIONING

NO CREDITCARDS
DOGS: PREFERABLY NOT
TAKEAWAY POSSIBLE
CATERING
MUSIC: CLASSICAL
IRANIAN
AMBIENCE: FOLKLORISTIC

A good example of the elaborate Persian cuisine, brought with style.

* Levant

€ **TURKISH**
9 WETERINGSCHANS 93
1017 RZ, CENTRUM
T/F 622 51 84
WWW.
RESTAURANTLEVANT.NL

OPEN 5 PM-MIDNIGHT,
CLOSED SUN
SEATING: 50
GROUPS: MAX. 50
TERRACE AT THE WATER-
SIDE
CATERING
MUSIC: WORLDMUSIC &

JAZZ
AMBIENCE: SIMPLE

A pleasant, simple Turkish restaurant.

Mamouche

€€ **MOROCCAN**
10 QUELLIJNSTRAAT 104
1072 XZ, OUD-ZUID
T 673 63 61
WWW.RESTAURANT
MAMOUCHE.NL

OPEN DAILY 6.30-10.30
PM
RESERVATION REC.
SEATING: 46
GROUPS: MAX. 15
NO DOGS
TERRACE
MUSIC: ARABIC LOUNGE

AMBIENCE: MODERN-
FOLKLORISTIC

A fancy Maghreb restaurant, a bit snug.

* Marrakech

€ **MOROCCAN**
11 NIEUWEZIJDS VOOR-
BURGWAL 134
1012 SH, CENTRUM
T 623 50 03

OPEN 4-10 PM,
CLOSED WED
RESERVATION REC.
SEATING: 50
GROUPS: MAX. 50
PRIVATE DINING ROOMS
TAKEAWAY POSSIBLE

CATERING
MUSIC: FOLKLORISTIC
AMBIENCE: FOLKLORISTIC

A weathered Moroccan restaurant with men in the kitchen.

** Paloma Blanca

€ **MOROCCAN**
12 JAN PIETER HEIJESTRAAT
145
1054 MG, OUD-WEST
T 612 64 85

OPEN 6-10 PM,
CLOSED MON
RESERVATION REC.
SEATING: 38
TERRACE
NO CREDITCARDS
TAKEAWAY POSSIBLE

CATERING
MUSIC: ARAB
AMBIENCE: SIMPLE-FOLK-
LORISTIC

Authentic Moroccan: mother does the cooking!

* Pygma-lion

€€ **SOUTH-AFRICAN**
13 NIEUWE SPIEGEL-
STRAAT 5 A
1017 DB, CENTRUM
T 420 70 22
WWW.PYGMA-LION.COM

OPEN 5.30-11 PM,
CLOSED MON
RESERVATION REC.
SEATING: 34
GROUPS: MAX. 30
TERRACE: UNDER THE
GALLERY
NO SMOKING, ONLY ON

THE TERRACE
CATERING
MUSIC: WORLDMUSIC
AMBIENCE: MODERN

Well-groomed food, and in stylish surroundings.

Zina

€€ **MOROCCAN/TUNESIAN**
14 BOSBOOM TOUSSAINT-
STRAAT 70
1054 AV, OUD-WEST
T 489 37 07 / F 489 37 22

OPEN TUE-SUN 6.30-
10 PM, CLOSED MON
RESERVATION REC.
SEATING: 40
GROUPS: MAX. 20
BAR
TERRACE

MUSIC: ARAB
AMBIENCE: MODERN

The Maghreb with fantasy and adventure.

AMSTERDAM SURROUNDINGS

** Het Arsenaal

€€€ **FRENCH – HAUTE CUISINE**
KOOLTJESBUURT 1
1411 RZ NAARDEN
T (035) 695 11 49 / 694 91 48
F (035) 694 03 69
WWW.PAULFAGEL.NL

OPEN LUNCH MON-FRI
12 NOON-2 PM, DINNER
DAILY 6-10 PM
RESERVATION REC.
SEATING: 100
GROUPS: MAX. 300

PRIVATE DINING ROOMS
TERRACE
AIRCONDITIONING
CATERING
MUSIC: JAZZ-CLASSICAL
AMBIENCE: MODERN

The place to be seen.

** Ron Blaauw

€€€ **FRENCH – HAUTE CUISINE**
KERKSTRAAT 56
1191 JE OUDERKERK AAN
DE AMSTEL
T (020) 496 19 43
F (020) 496 57 01
WWW.RONBLAAUW.NL

OPEN TUE-FRI 12 NOON-
2 PM, TUE-SAT 6-10 PM
RESERVATION REC.
SEATING: 60
GROUPS: MAX. 30
PRIVATE DINING ROOMS
TERRACE
NO MUSIC

AMBIENCE: LUXURIOUS

Excellent French food in rustic village.

* Het Heerenhuis

€€€ **FRENCH – HAUTE CUISINE**
RIJPERWEG 83
1462 MD MIDDENBEEM-
STER
T (0299) 68 20 10
F (0299) 68 20 20
WWW.HETHEERENHUIS.NL

OPEN 12 NOON-9.30 PM,
CLOSED TUE, BUT
GROUPS ON REQUEST
RESERVATION REC.
SEATING: 75
GROUPS: MAX. 150
PRIVATE DINING ROOMS
TERRACE
WHEELCHAIRS

TOILET FACILITIES FOR
THE DISABLED
AMBIENCE: LUXURIOUS
MUSIC: CLASSICAL/
JAZZY, BACKGROUND

The Mansion; good French food.

Lambermon's

€€ **FRENCH**
SPAARNE 96
2011 CL HAARLEM
T (023) 542 78 04
F (023) 542 78 26
WWW.LAMBERMONS.NL

OPEN 6-11 PM,
CLOSED MON
RESERVATION REC.
SEATING: 85
GROUPS: MAX. 20
AIRCONDITIONING
(IN THE BACK)
MUSIC: LOUNGE

AMBIENCE: MODERN

Special formula in industrial landmark.

* Lute

€€€ **FRENCH – HAUTE CUISINE**
DE OUDE MOLEN 5
1184 VX OUDERKERK AAN
DE AMSTEL
T (020) 472 24 62
F (020) 472 24 63
WWW.LUTERESTAURANT.NL

OPEN LUNCH MON-FRI
12.30-3 PM, DINNER MON-
SUN 6.30-10 PM
RESERVATION REC.
SEATING: 100
GROUPS: MAX. 50
BAR, LOUNGE
TERRACE
AIRCONDITIONING

PRIVATE DINING ROOMS
8 & 14, VERANDAH 36
NO DOGS
MOORING IN RIVER
AMSTEL
NO MUSIC
AMBIENCE: MODERN

Another industrial landmark with refined food.

** Mario Uva

€€ **ITALIAN**
NECK 15
1456 AA WIJDEWORMER
T (0299) 42 39 49
WWW.MARIOUVA.NL

OPEN 7-11 PM,CLOSED
SUN, LUNCH ONLY ON
DEMAND
RESERVATION REC.
SEATING: 55
GROUPS: MAX. 60
SMOKING: ONLY IN THE

LOBBY
NO DOGS
AIRCONDITIONING
CATERING
MUSIC: BACKGROUND
ITALIAN
AMBIENCE: WELL-KEPT

The best Italian north of Ventimiglia?

* De Nederlanden

€€€ **FRENCH – HAUTE CUISINE**
DUINKERKEN 3
3633 EM VREELAND AAN DE
VECHT
T (0294) 23 23 26
F (0294) 23 14 07
WWW.NEDERLANDEN.NL

OPEN LUNCH MON-FRI
12 NOON-2 PM (SAT & SUN
ON REQUEST), DINNER
MON-SUN 6-9.30 PM
RESERVATION REC.
SEATING: 60
GROUPS: MAX. 60
TERRACE
PRIVATE DINING ROOMS:

6-40
NO DOGS
MOORING
MUSIC: LIGHT CLASSICAL
AMBIENCE: ROMANTIC

Beautiful riverside mansion with excellent food.

** Groot Paardenburg

€€€ **FRENCH – HAUTE CUISINE**
AMSTELZIJDE 55
1184 TZ OUDERKERK AAN
DE AMSTEL
T (020) 496 12 10 /
F (020) 496 91 09
WWW.ENGELGROEP.COM

OPEN LUNCH MON-FRI
12 NOON-3 PM, DINNER
MON-SAT 6-10 PM,
CLOSED SUN.
RESERVATION REC.
SEATING: 85
GROUPS MAX. 150
TERRACE
AIRCONDITIONING
PRIVATE DINING ROOMS

VALET PARKING WED-SAT
DOGS: RATHER NOT
CATERING
MUSIC : LOUNGE/BACK-
GROUND
AMBIENCE: LUXURIOUS

For the lovers of excellent meat in a stylish, roomy riverside restaurant.

Klein Paardenburg

€€ FRENCH – MIDDLE CLASS
AMSTELZIJDE 55
1184 TZ OUDERKERK A/D
AMSTEL
T (020) 496 12 10 /
F (020) 496 91 09
WWW.ENGELGROEP.COM

OPEN DAILY 12 NOON-
3 PM AND 6-10.30 PM;
NO LUNCH ON SAT
RESERVATION REC.
SEATING: 60
GROUPS: MAX. 80
TERRACE OVER THE RIVER
AIRCONDITIONING
MOORING

MUSIC: BACKGROUND
AMBIENCE: MODERN

Nice.

* De Rijsttafel

€ INDONESIAN
KRUISWEG 70 D
2011 LG HAARLEM
T (023) 534 34 56
WWW.REST-DE-
RIJSTTAFEL.NL

OPEN 6-10 PM, CLOSED
MON, BUT GROUPS ON
DEMAND
RESERVATION REC.
SEATING: 32
GROUPS: MAX. 32
AIRCONDITIONING
CATERING

MUSIC: INDONESIAN,
BACKGROUND
AMBIENCE: FOLKLORISTIC

Fine Indonesian restaurant; ask for the dry rendang asli!

* De Vrienden van Jacob

€€€ FRENCH – HAUTE CUISINE
DUIN EN KRUIDBERGER-
WEG 60
2071 LE SANTPOORT
T (023) 512 18 00
F (023) 512 18 88
WWW.DUIN-KRUIDBERG.NL

OPEN 6-9.30 PM,
CLOSED SUN
RESERVATION REC.
SEATING: 40
GROUPS: MAX. 8
BAR
TERRACE
PRIVATE DINING ROOMS
NO DOGS
MUSIC:

CLASSICAL/BACKGROUND
AMBIENCE: STYLISH

French cuisine in Holland's largest mansion in a beautiful landscape.

*** Wilhelminapark

€€€ FRENCH – HAUTE CUISINE
WILHELMINAPARK 65
3581 NP UTRECHT
T (030) 251 06 93
F (030) 254 07 64
WWW.WILHELMINAPARK.NL

OPEN LUNCH MON-FRI
12 NOON-2 PM, DINNER
MON-SAT 6-9.30 PM
RESERVATION REC.:
DURING OFFICE-HOURS
SEATING: 65
GROUPS: MAX. 24
TERRACE

PRIVATE DINING ROOMS:
24
NO MUSIC
AMBIENCE: QUIET CHIC

Subtle tastes in park-like surroundings.

ASIAN

* A-Fusion

€ ASIAN FUSION
15 ZEEDIJK 130
1012 BC, CENTRUM
T 330 40 68 / F 330 40 66

OPEN DAILY 12 NOON-
11 PM
RESERVATION REC. AT
WEEKENDS
SEATING: 60
GROUPS: MAX. 20
BAR

AIRCONDITIONING
DOGS: ASK FIRST
TAKEAWAY POSSIBLE
CATERING
MUSIC: ORIENTAL DVD'S
AMBIENCE: MODERN
LOUNGE

Fast or slow, nice and tasty.

Arirang

€€ KOREAN
[16] MARNIXSTRAAT 198
1016 TJ, CENTRUM
T 620 09 62 / F 427 05 02

OPEN 6-11 PM,
CLOSED TUE
RESERVATION REC.
SEATING: 42
GROUPS: MAX. 25
PRIVATE DINING ROOMS
BAR

AIRCONDITIONING: ONLY
UPSTAIRS
TAKEAWAY POSSIBLE: LI-
MITED
MUSIC: FOLKLORISTIC
AMBIENCE: SIMPLE-FOLK-
LORISTIC

For the lovers of Korean food.

** Dynasty

€€€ ASIAN
[17] REGULIERSDWARSSTRAAT
30
1017 BM, CENTRUM
T 626 84 00 / F 622 30 38
WWW.
DYNASTYRESTAURANT.NL

OPEN 5.30-10.30 PM,
CLOSED TUE
RESERVATION REC.
SEATING: 90
GROUPS: MAX. 30
PRIVATE DINING ROOMS
BAR
TERRACE / GARDEN
NO DOGS

AIRCONDITIONING
CASH PAYMENT ONLY
MUSIC: MIXED
AMBIENCE: FOLKLORISTIC

Posh and comfortable Pan-Asiatic.

* The Himalaya

€ INDIAN
[18] HAARLEMMERSTRAAT 11
1013 EH, CENTRUM
T 622 37 76 / F 625 02 41

OPEN DAILY 5-11.30 PM
RESERVATION REC.
SEATING: 45
GROUPS: MAX. 45
BAR
TAKEAWAY POSSIBLE

CATERING
MUSIC: CLASSICAL-FOLK-
LORISTIC
AMBIENCE: FOLKLORISTIC

Punjabi family cooks traditionally.

Kong Kha

€ THAI
[19] RIJNSTRAAT 87
1079 GZ, ZUIDERAMSTEL
T 661 25 78

OPEN 4-9.45 PM,
CLOSED MON
RESERVATION REC.
SEATING: 32
GROUPS: MAX. 10
BAR

TERRACE
TAKEAWAY POSSIBLE
NO DOGS
CASH PAYMENT ONLY
MUSIC: THAI
AMBIENCE: VERY SIMPLE

Almost a snackbar, but good quality.

De Kooning van Siam

€€ THAI
[20] OUDEZIJDS VOORBURGWAL
42
1012 GE, CENTRUM
T 623 72 93 / F 0226-345 491
WWW.DEKOONINGVAN-
SIAM.NL

OPEN 6-10.30 PM,
CLOSED SUN
RESERVATION REC.
SEATING: 45
GROUPS: MAX. 50
PRIVATE DINING ROOMS
MUSIC: THAI
AMBIENCE: FOLKLORISTIC

A glittering Thai.

** Memories of India

€€ **INDIAN**

21 REGULIERSDWARS-
STRAAT 88
1017 BN, CENTRUM
T 623 57 10
WWW.
MEMORIESOFINDIA.NL

OPEN DAILY 5-11.30 PM
RESERVATION REC. AT
WEEKENDS
SEATING: 78
GROUPS: MAX. 70
BAR
NO DOGS
TAKEAWAY POSSIBLE
MUSIC: INDIAN
AMBIENCE: MODERN-

FOLKLORISTIC

Indian food like in London.

* Me Naam Naan

€€ **THAI**

22 KONINGSSTRAAT 29
1011 ET, CENTRUM
T 423 33 44 / F 423 08 68

OPEN 4-10.30 PM,
CLOSED MON
RESERVATION REC.
SEATING: 45
GROUPS: MAX. 25
PRIVATE DINING ROOMS

CATERING
TAKEAWAY POSSIBLE
CASH PAYMENT ONLY
MUSIC: THAI
AMBIENCE: SIMPLE

A simple but excellent Thai.

** Pakistan

€€ **PAKISTANI**

23 SCHELDESTRAAT 100
1078 GP, ZUIDERAMSTEL
T 675 39 76

OPEN DAILY 5-11 PM
SEATING: 56
GROUPS: MAX. 60
CASH PAYMENT ONLY
TERRACE
TAKEAWAY POSSIBLE

CATERING
MUSIC: INDIAN
AMBIENCE: SIMPLE-
ROMANTIC

Very good Pakistani cuisine.

Tagore

€ **NORTH-INDIAN**

24 UTRECHTSESTRAAT 128
1017 VT, CENTRUM
T 624 19 31 / F 646 08 15

OPEN DAILY 4-11 PM
RESERVATION REC.
SEATING: 40
GROUPS: MAX. 40
TAKEAWAY POSSIBLE
CATERING

MUSIC: CLASSICAL
INDIAN
AMBIENCE: SIMPLE-
ROMANTIC

Simple North-Indian food.

Take Thai

€€ **THAI**

25 UTRECHTSESTRAAT 87
1017 VK, CENTRUM
T 622 05 77

OPEN DAILY 6-10.30 PM
RESERVATION REC.
SEATING: 40
GROUPS: MAX. 10
MUSIC: THAI POP
AMBIENCE: MODERN

Fancy Thai for yuppies.

Tashi Deleg

€ **TIBETAN + INDONESIAN**

26 UTRECHTSESTRAAT 65
1017 VJ, CENTRUM
T 620 66 24

OPEN DAILY 4-11 PM
RESERVATION REC. AT
WEEKENDS
SEATING: 38
GROUPS: MAX. 35
BAR

CREDITCARDS: ONLY VISA
CATERING
MUSIC: TIBETAN
AMBIENCE: FOLKLORISTIC

A fair Tibetan, now also Indonesion food from the neighbours (Tujuh Maret).

Top Thai

€€ **THAI**
27 HERENSTRAAT 22
1015 CB, CENTRUM
T 623 46 33
F (023) 531 44 36
WWW.TOPTHAI.NL

OPEN DAILY 4.30-10.30
PM
RESERVATION REC.
SEATING: 30
GROUPS: MAX. 30
BAR
AIRCONDITIONING
TAKEAWAY POSSIBLE

CATERING
MUSIC: FOLKLORISTIC
AMBIENCE: SIMPLE-
FOLKLORISTIC

A reasonably small Thai.

Wagamama

€ **ASIAN**
28 MAX EUWEPLEIN 10
1017 MB, CENTRUM
T 528 77 78
WWW.WAGAMAMA.NL

OPEN SUN-WED 12 NOON-
10 PM, THU-SAT 12 NOON-
11 PM
SEATING: 150
GROUPS: MAX. 14
AIRCONDITIONING
NO SMOKING

NO DOGS
TERRACE
TAKEAWAY POSSIBLE
NO MUSIC
AMBIENCE: MODERN DINER

Successful international formula, nice for the kids.

* Wau

€ **MALAYSIAN**
29 ZEEDIJK 35
1012 AR, CENTRUM
T 421 24 87
WWW.WAU.NU

OPEN DAILY 5-11 PM
RESERVATION REC.
SEATING: 40
GROUPS: MAX. 40
BAR
MUSIC: NATURE SOUNDS

AMBIENCE: MODERN-
ROMANTIC

Simpel Malaysian; halal.

* White Elephant

€€ **THAI**
30 VAN WOUSTRAAT 3
1074 AA, OUD-ZUID
T 679 55 56 / F 679 55 58
WWW.WHITEELEPHANT.NL

OPEN 3-11 PM,
CLOSED MON
RESERVATION REC.
SEATING: 43
GROUPS: MAX. 18
TERRACE: IN THE GARDEN
NO DOGS

TAKEAWAY POSSIBLE
CATERING
MUSIC: THAI
AMBIENCE: WELL-KEPT

Best Thai in town.

CAFÉ-RESTAURANT

* Bern

€ **SWISS**
31 NIEUWMARKT 9
1011 JR, CENTRUM
T 622 00 34

OPEN 4 PM-1 AM, DINNER
6-11 PM
RESERVATION REC.
SEATING: 50
GROUPS: MAX. 22
BAR

CASH PAYMENT ONLY
NO MUSIC
AMBIENCE: SIMPLE

A pub with Swiss pubfood, cheese fondue, steak etc.

Dantzig aan de Amstel

€€ **INTERNATIONAL**
32 ZWANENBURGWAL 15
1011 VW, CENTRUM
T 620 90 39 / F 620 90 41

OPEN LUNCH 11 AM-5 PM,
DINNER 5.30-10 PM
RESERVATION REC.
SEATING: 130
GROUPS: MAX. 100
BAR
TERRACE

MUSIC: JAZZ-POP-CLAS-
SICAL, BACKGROUND
AMBIENCE: MODERN-
INFORMAL

Because it's there, near the opera.

De Doffer

€ RUNSTRAAT 12-14
33 | 1016 GK, CENTRUM
T 622 66 86
WWW.DOFFER.COM

OPEN LUNCH 12 NOON-
3 PM,
DINNER 6-10 PM
SEATING: 44
GROUPS: MAX. 30
PRIVATE DINING ROOMS

BAR
TERRACE
MUSIC: JAZZ-POP
AMBIENCE: CLASSIC PUB

Simple pub fare.

De Reiger

€ NIEUWE LELIESTRAAT 34
34 | 1015 ST, CENTRUM
T 624 74 26

OPEN LUNCH SAT-SUN
11 AM-3.30 PM,
DINNER DAILY 6-10.30 PM
RESERVATION REC. ONLY
FOR LUNCH
SEATING: 68
GROUPS: MAX. 10

BAR
NO CREDITCARDS
NO MUSIC
NO-SMOKING AREA AT
NIGHT
AMBIENCE: INFORMAL

Successful noisy pub with excellent fare.

* La Vallade

€ FRENCH –
35 | MEDITERRANEAN
RINGDIJK 23
1097 AB, OOST/
WATERGRAAFSMEER
T/F 665 20 25

OPEN DAILY 6-10 PM
RESERVATION REC.
SEATING: 55
GROUPS: MAX. 8
BAR
TERRACE
NO-SMOKING AREA
NO CREDITCARDS

MUSIC: JAZZ-CLASSICAL-
FOLKLORISTIC-FRENCH
AMBIENCE: SIMPLE-
FRENCH

Very popular, international pub food.

Vertigo

€€ INTERNATIONAL
36 | VONDELPARK 3 (NEXT TO
FILMMUSEUM)
1071 AA, OUD-ZUID
T 612 30 21 / F 681 20 21
WWW.VERTIGO.NL

OPEN LUNCH 10 AM-5 PM,
DINNER 6-10 PM
SEATING: 55
GROUPS: MAX. 25
BAR
TERRACE: COVERED AND
HEATED
CATERING

MUSIC: JAZZ-POP-
CLASSICAL
AMBIENCE: INFORMAL

Nice terrace, reasonable food.

CHINESE

Nam Kee

€ CANTONESE
37 | ZEEDIJK 111
1012 AV, CENTRUM
T 624 34 70 / F 639 30 48
WWW.NAMKEE.NL

OPEN MON-SAT 12 NOON-
11 PM,
SUN 12 NOON-10 PM
SEATING: 80
GROUPS: MAX. 30
AIRCONDITIONING
TAKEAWAY POSSIBLE

NO CREDITCARDS
MUSIC: FOLKLORISTIC
AMBIENCE: SIMPLE

Oldfashioned, simple Chinese.

Nam Kee

€ CANTONESE
38 | GELDERSEKADE 117
1011 EN, CENTRUM
T 639 28 48 / F 639 30 48
WWW.NAMKEE.NL

OPEN DAILY 12 NOON-
00.30 AM
RESERVATION REC. AT
WEEKEND
SEATING: 80
GROUPS: MAX. 30
AIRCONDITIONING

TAKEAWAY POSSIBLE
MUSIC: FOLKLORISTIC
AMBIENCE: SIMPLE

Oldfashioned simple Chinese fishdishes.

* New King

€€ ZEEDIJK 115-117
39 1012 AV, CENTRUM
T 625 21 80
WWW.NEWKING.NL

OPEN DAILY 11 AM-
MIDNIGHT
RESERVATION REC.
SEATING: 140
PRIVATE DINING ROOMS
CATERING

TAKEAWAY POSSIBLE
MUSIC: CHINESE
AMBIENCE: SIMPLE

No-nonsense restaurant, also takeaway possible.

* Oriental City

€€ **CANTONESE**
40 OUDEZIJDS VOORBURG-
WAL 177-179
1012 EV, CENTRUM
T 626 83 52 / F 626 92 95
WWW.ORIENTAL-CITY.NL

OPEN DAILY 11.30 AM-
10.30 PM,
DIM SUM 11.30 AM-4.30
PM
RESERVATION REC.
SEATING: 230
GROUPS: MAX. 70
AIRCONDITIONING

CATERING
LUNCH MENU
DIM SUM
MUSIC: MUZAK-FOLKLO-
RISTIC
AMBIENCE: FOLKLORISTIC

Specialised in dim sum.

Sea Palace

€€€ OOSTERDOKSKADE 8
41 1011 AD, CENTRUM
T 626 47 77
F 620 42 66
WWW.SEAPALACE.NL

OPEN DAILY 12 NOON-
11 PM
RESERVATION REC.
SEATING: 700
GROUPS: MAX. 700
BAR
NO DOGS
TOILET FACILITIES FOR

THE DISABLED
MOORING
AIRCONDITIONING
TAKEAWAY POSSIBLE
LUNCH MENU
DIM SUM
MUSIC: FOLKLORISTIC
AMBIENCE: FOLKLORISTIC

Big, bigger, biggest. Both posh and mid-price.

* Sichuan Food

€€ REGULIERSDWARSSTRAAT
42 35
1017 BK, CENTRUM
T 626 93 27 / F 627 72 81

OPEN DAILY 5.30-10.30
PM
RESERVATION REC.
SEATING: 38
GROUPS: MAX. 26
PRIVATE DINING ROOMS

NO DOGS
AIRCONDITIONING
CASH PAYMENT ONLY
MUSIC: FOLKLORISTIC
AMBIENCE: CLASSIC-
FOLKLORISTIC

Posh Chinese restaurant.

Tong Fa

€€ JOHAN HUIZINGALAAN
43 192
1065 JJ, SLOTERVAART/
OVERTOOMSE VELD
T 615 26 55 / F 617 80 75
WWW.TONGFA.NL

OPEN MON-FRI 12 NOON-
10 PM, SUN 4-10 PM,
CLOSED SAT
RESERVATION REC.
SEATING: 48
GROUPS: MAX. 20
BAR
NO DOGS

AIRCONDITIONING
TAKEAWAY POSSIBLE
MUSIC: CLASSICAL-FOLK-
LORISTIC
AMBIENCE: MODERN

Modernised Chinese.

DUTCH

** Greetje

€ PEPERSTRAAT 23
44 1011 TJ CENTRUM
T 779 74 50
WWW.RESTAURANT
GREETJE.NL

OPEN WED/THU/SUN 5-10
PM, FRI-SAT 5-11 PM,
CLOSED MON-TUE
RESERVATION REC.
SEATING: 55
GROUPS: MAX. 55
BAR

AIRCONDITIONING
NO CREDITCARDS
MUSIC: BACKGROUND
AMBIENCE: OLD DUTCH

Very well treated original Dutch food in a nice ambience.

De Keuken van 1870

€ SPUISTRAAT 4
45 1012 TS, CENTRUM
T 620 40 18
WWW.KEUKENVAN1870.NL

OPEN MON-SAT 5-10 PM,
CLOSED SUN, BUT
GROUPS BY APPOINT-
MENT
SEATING: 75
GROUPS: MAX. 40
TERRACE

AIRCONDITIONING
CASH PAYMENT ONLY
TAKEAWAY POSSIBLE
MUSIC: JAZZ
AMBIENCE: SIMPLE

Modern version of the old soup kitchen. And not just soup!

* De Roode Leeuw

€€ DAMRAK 93-94
46 1012 LP, CENTRUM
T 555 06 66 / F 620 47 16
WWW.
HOTELAMSTERDAM.NL

OPEN DAILY 12 NOON-
10 PM
RESERVATION REC.
SEATING: 65
GROUPS: MAX. 90
TERRACE: GLASSHOUSE,
WITH WIFI

AIRCONDITIONING
NO MUSIC
AMBIENCE: SIMPLE-
CLASSIC

For dining in old Dutch style in the heart of Amsterdam.

Piet de Leeuw

€ NOORDERSTRAAT 11
47 1017 TR, CENTRUM
T/F 623 71 81
WWW.PIETDELEEUW.NL

OPEN MON-FRI 12 NOON-
11 PM, SAT-SUN 5-11 PM
SEATING: 75
GROUPS: MAX. 35
MUSIC: AMSTERDAM
FOLKLORISTIC

AMBIENCE: SIMPLE

Real Dutch pub food, especially steak.

EUROPEAN

* Aleksandar

€€ GRILL – MEDITERRANEAN
48 CEINTUURBAAN 196
1072 GC, OUD-ZUID
T 676 63 84 / F 671 00 20

OPEN DAILY 5-10 PM
RESERVATION REC.
SEATING: 80
GROUPS: MAX. 85
PRIVATE DINING ROOMS
BAR

MUSIC: MEDITERRANEAN
AMBIENCE: CLASSIC-
FOLKLORISTIC

Authentic Balkan restaurant.

** Casa Juan

€ SPANISH
49 LINDENGRACHT 59
1015 KC, CENTRUM
T 623 78 38

OPEN 6-11 PM
CLOSED MON & TUE
RESERVATION REC.
SEATING: 24
GROUPS: MAX. 12
BAR

TERRACE
NO DOGS
MUSIC: SPANISH
AMBIENCE: FOLKLORISTIC

As if you are in Spain, small, smelly, but good.

* Centra

€ SPANISH
50 LANGE NIEZEL 29
1012 GS, CENTRUM
T 622 30 50 / F 453 39 79

OPEN DAILY 1-11 PM
RESERVATION REC.
SEATING: 66
GROUPS: MAX. 10
BAR
NO DOGS

NO CREDITCARDS
MUSIC: FOLKLORISTIC
AMBIENCE: SIMPLE

Large, simple, and very Spanish.

* Grekas

€ **GREEK**
51 SINGEL 311
1012 WJ, CENTRUM
T 620 35 90

OPEN 1-9.30 PM,
CLOSED MON & TUE
RESERVATION REC.
SEATING: 10
NO DOGS
TAKEAWAY POSSIBLE

CASH PAYMENT ONLY
MUSIC: POP-FOLKLO-
RISTIC
AMBIENCE: SIMPLE-
MEDITERRANEAN

Takeaway possible with a few chairs, always excellent.

De Griekse
Taverna

€ **GREEK**
52 HOBBEMAKADE 64-65
1071 XM, OUD-ZUID
T 671 79 23

OPEN LUNCH 12 NOON-
4 PM,
DINNER 5-11 PM
SEATING: 75
GROUPS: MAX. 80
CATERING
BAR

TERRACE
NO CREDITCARDS
MUSIC: GREEK, SOMETI-
MES LIVE
AMBIENCE: INFORMAL

Large Greek taverna; simple but good food.

* Nostos

€ **GREEK**
53 WESTERSTRAAT 40
1015 MK, CENTRUM
T 626 28 32

OPEN 5-10 PM,
CLOSED TUE
RESERVATION REC.
SEATING: 35
GROUPS: MAX. 40
TERRACE: SMALL

CASH PAYMENT ONLY
MUSIC: GREEK
AMBIENCE: SIMPLE

Small and noisy; excellent Thessaloniki food.

Polonia

€ **POLISH – RUSSIAN**
54 DERDE OOSTERPARK-
STRAAT 72
1091 KA, OOST/
WATERGRAAFSMEER
T 663 26 25

OPEN TUE-SUN 5.30 PM,
LUNCH (& DINNER ON
MON) BY APPOINTMENT
SEATING: 32
GROUPS: MAX. 32
AIRCONDITIONING
TAKEAWAY POSSIBLE ON
REQUEST

MUSIC: POLISH-RUSSIAN,
SOMETIMES LIVE
AMBIENCE: CLASSIC-
FOLKLORISTIC

Homely cooking, served with insanity.

Portugália

€ **PORTUGUESE**
55 KERKSTRAAT 35
1017 GB, CENTRUM
T 625 64 90
WWW.PORTUGALIA.NL

OPEN MON-WED 5 PM-
MIDNIGHT, THU-SUN
1 PM-MIDNIGHT
RESERVATION REC.
SEATING: 65
NO DOGS
BAR

AIRCONDITIONING
CATERING
MUSIC: MIXED,
SOMETIMES LIVE (FADO)
AMBIENCE: SIMPLE-
ROMANTIC-HOMELY

Touristy but good food.

* Prego

€€ **MEDITERRANEAN**
56 HERENSTRAAT 25
1015 BZ, CENTRUM
T 638 01 48
WWW.
PREGORESTAURANT.NL

OPEN 6-10 PM,
IN SUMMER UNTIL
10.30 PM
RESERVATION REC.
SEATING: 34
GROUPS: 40
NO MUSIC
AMBIENCE: MODERN

Modern and simple food and surroundings.

** La Sala

€ **SPANISH / PORTUGUESE**
57 PLANTAGE KERKLAAN 41
1018 CV, CENTRUM
T 624 48 46

OPEN 4 PM-MIDNIGHT,
CLOSED MON
RESERVATION REC.
SEATING: 50
GROUPS: MAX. 12
TERRACE

NO CREDITCARDS
CATERING
MUSIC: TANGO,
SOUTH-AMERICAN
AMBIENCE: SIMPLE

Large, noisy, authentic.

Tapas Bar Català

€ **CATALAN**
58 SPUISTRAAT 299
1012 VS, CENTRUM
T 623 11 41

OPEN MON-THU 4 PM-
MIDNIGHT,
FRI 4 PM-1 AM, SAT-SUN
1 PM-1 AM
SEATING: 24
BAR

TERRACE
CATERING
NO CREDITCARDS
NO MUSIC
AMBIENCE: SIMPLE

Just what the name suggests.

Vamos a ver

€€ **SPANISH**
59 GOVERT FLINCK-
STRAAT 308
1073 CJ, OUD-ZUID
T 673 69 92

OPEN 5.30-10.30 PM,
CLOSED TUE
RESERVATION REC.
SEATING: 40
GROUPS: MAX. 40
BAR
NO CREDITCARDS

PRIVATE DINING ROOMS
TAKEAWAY POSSIBLE
CATERING
MUSIC: SPANISH
AMBIENCE: RUSTIC

Cosy and personal Spanish food.

FISH

Albatros Seafoodhouse

€€ WESTERSTRAAT 264
60 1051 MT, CENTRUM
T 627 99 32 / F 626 12 20
WWW.RESTAURANT
ALBATROS.NL

OPEN 6 PM-MIDNIGHT,
CLOSED TUE & WED
RESERVATION REC.
SEATING: 42
GROUPS: MAX. 45
NO-SMOKING AREA
MUSIC: SEASOUNDS
TERRACE: SERRE

AMBIENCE: SIMPLE-
CLASSIC-ROMANTIC

A nice fish restaurant, nothing fancy, but they take care of non-smokers.

* Brasserie Bark

€€ VAN BAERLESTRAAT 120
61 1071 BD, OUD-ZUID
T 675 02 10 / F 642 42 73
WWW.BARK.NL

OPEN LUNCH MON-FRI
12 NOON-3 PM, DINNER
DAILY 5.30 PM-00.30 AM
RESERVATION REC.
SEATING: 56
GROUPS: MAX. 25

TERRACE
AIRCONDITIONING
MUSIC: BACKGROUND
AMBIENCE: MODERN

Like a French brasserie, specialized in seafood, open till midnight.

* Eénvistwéévis

€ SCHIPPERSGRACHT 6
62 1011 TR, CENTRUM
T 623 28 94

OPEN 6-10 PM,
CLOSED MON
RESERVATION REC.
SEATING: 28
GROUPS: MAX. 10

MOORING
MUSIC: SPANISH
AMBIENCE: SIMPLE

Small, very personal fish restaurant.

Lucius

€€ SPUISTRAAT 247
63 1012 VP, CENTRUM
T 624 18 31 / F 627 61 53
WWW.LUCIUS.NL

OPEN DAILY 5 PM-
MIDNIGHT
RESERVATION REC.
SEATING: 75
GROUPS: MAX. 20
BAR

TERRACE
MOORING AT SINGEL
CANAL
NO MUSIC
AMBIENCE: SIMPLE

A classical informal, brasserie-type fish restaurant.

* Vis aan
de Schelde

€€€ SCHELDEPLEIN 4
64 1078 GR, ZUIDERAMSTEL
T 675 15 83 / F 670 46 17
WWW.
VISAANDESCHELDE.NL

OPEN LUNCH
MON-FRI 12 NOON-
2.30 PM,
DINNER 5.30-11 PM
RESERVATION NECESSARY
SEATING: 60
GROUPS: MAX. 12
TERRACE

VALET PARKING
MUSIC: BACKGROUND
AMBIENCE: MODERN
COMFORTABLE

The best specialized fish restaurant in town. Always make a reservation!

FRENCH – SIMPLE

* Amsterdam

€ **CAFÉ-RESTAURANT**
65 WATERTORENPLEIN 6
1051 PA, WESTERPARK
T 682 26 66 / F 682 26 65
WWW.CRADAM.NL

OPEN 11 AM-10.30 PM,
FRI & SAT 11 AM-11.30 PM
RESERVATION REC.
SEATING: 270
GROUPS: MAX. 50
BAR
TERRACE

NO MUSIC
AMBIENCE: SIMPLE

Huge Chartier wannabe, very popular.

* Côte Ouest

€ GRAVENSTRAAT 20
66 1012 NM, CENTRUM
T 320 89 98
F 427 25 05
WWW.COTEOUEST.NL

OPEN TUE-SUN 5-10 PM,
CLOSED MON
RESERVATION REC.
SEATING: 52
GROUPS: MAX. 8
BAR
TERRACE

CREDITCARDS: ONLY
MASTER/VISA/MAESTRO
NO-SMOKING AREA
DOGS: PREFERABLY NOT
MUSIC: FRENCH
AMBIENCE: RURAL
FRENCH

The French West Coast serves pancakes and good brasserie food. Try the excellent cider!

* À la Ferme

€€ GOVERT FLINCK-
67 STRAAT 251
1073 BX, OUD-ZUID
T 679 82 40 / F 679 30 92
WWW.ALAFERME.NL

OPEN 6-10 PM,
CLOSED SUN & MON
RESERVATION REC.
SEATING: 45
GROUPS: MAX. 16
TERRACE: PATIO
PRIVATE DINING ROOMS

NO CREDITCARDS
MUSIC: SOUTH-AMERI-
CAN, JAZZ, FADO
AMBIENCE: POSTMODERN

Simple but nice cuisine.

* De Gouden
Reael

€€ **FRENCH-REGIONAL**
68 ZANDHOEK 14
1013 KT, CENTRUM
T 623 38 83 / F 625 73 17
WWW.GOUDENREAEL.NL

OPEN LUNCH
MON-FRI 11 AM-4 PM,
SAT-SUN 12 NOON-4 PM,
DINNER 6-11 PM
RESERVATION REC.
SEATING: 60
GROUPS: MAX. 18
PRIVATE DINING ROOMS

BAR
MUSIC: FRENCH
AMBIENCE: INFORMAL

French regional cuisine in Dutch picturesque surroundings near the harbour.

De Luwte

€ LELIEGRACHT 26-28
69 1015 DG, CENTRUM
T 625 85 48 / F 428 77 83
WWW.
RESTAURANTDELUWTE.NL

OPEN LUNCH TUE-SUN
11 AM-3.30 PM, DINNER
DAILY 6-10 PM
SEATING: 46
GROUPS: MAX. 10
TERRACE
MUSIC: FRENCH/SPANISH

AMBIENCE: ROMANTIC,
PATIO-INTERIOR

Simple and cosy.

Marius

€ BARENTSZSTRAAT 243
70 1013 NM, CENTRUM
T 422 78 80

OPEN 6-10 PM,
CLOSED SUN & MON
RESERVATION REC.
SEATING: 24
GROUPS: MAX. 24

TERRACE
NO MUSIC
AMBIENCE: SIMPLE

Former Alice Waters assistant (Chez Panisse) cooks simple, excellent Mediterranean-style food.

** Le Petit Latin

€€ **MEDITERRANEAN**
71 NIEUWEZIJDS VOOR-
BURGWAL 306
1012 RV, CENTRUM
T 624 94 25

OPEN FROM 7 PM UNTIL
THE BOSS SAYS IT'S TIME
TO GO, CLOSED SUN &
MON
RESERVATION REC.
SEATING: 30
GROUPS: MAX. 18

MUSIC: FRENCH
AMBIENCE: SIMPLE-
ROMANTIC

Very personal provincial cuisine. The chef is from Marseille.

* Vondelkade

€ OVERTOOM 109
72 1054 HD, OUD-WEST
T 689 30 03
WWW.VONDELKADE.NL

OPEN 6-10.30 PM,
CLOSED SUN & MON
RESERVATION REC.
SEATING: 32
GROUPS: MAX. 8
NO MUSIC

AMBIENCE: SOBER

Very simple eatery.

FRENCH — AVERAGE

* Brasserie Van Baerle

€€ VAN BAERLESTRAAT 158
74 1071 BG, OUD-ZUID
T 679 15 32 / F 671 71 96
WWW.
BRASSERIEVANBAERLE.NL

OPEN MON-FRI 12 NOON-
11 PM,
SAT 5.30-11 PM, SUN 10
AM-11 PM
RESERVATION REC.
SEATING: 50
GROUPS: MAX. 42
PRIVATE DINING ROOMS

TERRACE: IN THE GARDEN
MUSIC: JAZZ-CLASSICAL
AMBIENCE: BRASSERIE

A reliable lunch and dinner restaurant, with a nice garden terrace.

* Breitner

€€ AMSTEL 212
75 1017 AH, CENTRUM
T 627 78 79 / F 330 29 98
WWW.RESTAURANT-
BREITNER.NL

OPEN 6-10.30 PM,
CLOSED SUN
RESERVATION REC.
SEATING: 48
GROUPS: MAX. 48
MOORING
MUSIC: MODERN, LIGHT

MUSIC
AMBIENCE: CLASSIC

Bring your mother-in-law and let her enjoy the spectacular view.

* Chez Georges

€€ HERENSTRAAT 3
76 1015 BX, CENTRUM
T 626 33 32 / F 638 78 38

OPEN 6-10.30 PM,
CLOSED SUN & WED
RESERVATION REC.
SEATING: 28
GROUPS: MAX. 7

AIRCONDITIONING
MUSIC: MUZAK
AMBIENCE: ROMANTIC

Usually called Belgian, but actually a bourgeois French restaurant.

Damsteeg

€€ REESTRAAT 28-32
77 1016 DN, CENTRUM
T 627 87 94 / F 623 87 49
WWW.DAMSTEEG.NL

OPEN 6-10.30 PM,
CLOSED SUN
RESERVATION REC.
SEATING: 59
GROUPS: MAX. 60
BAR WITH TAPAS
TERRACE

PRIVATE DINING ROOMS:
MAX. 26
MOORING AROUND THE
CORNER
MUSIC: FRENCH-JAZZ
AMBIENCE: CLASSIC

One of the nicest surroundings with decent food.

* Dauphine

€€ PRINS BERNHARDPLEIN
78 175
1097 BL, OOST-
WATERGRAAFSMEER
T 462 16 46
WWW.CAFERESTAURANT-
DAUPHINE.NL

OPEN MON-THU 8 AM-
10.30 PM, FRI 8 AM-
11.30 PM, SAT 10.30 AM-
11.30 PM, SUN 10.30 AM-
10.30 PM
RESERVATION REC.
SEATING: 210
GROUPS: MAX. 25
BAR

TERRACE
AIRCONDITIONING
PRIVATE DINING ROOM
NO-SMOKING AREA
NO MUSIC
AMBIENCE: MODERN

A huge room in what used to be a Renault-garage with good French brasserie food.

** Elkaar

€€ ALEXANDERPLEIN 6
79 1018 CG, CENTRUM
T 330 75 59
F 423 44 78
WWW.ETENBIJELKAAR.NL

OPEN DAILY 12 NOON-
2 PM AND 6-10 PM,
SAT NO LUNCH
RESERVATION REC.
SEATING: 35
GROUPS: MAX. 40
TERRACE

PRIVATE DINING ROOMS
MOORING
MUSIC: JAZZY, BACK-
GROUND
AMBIENCE: HIGH CLASS
FOOD IN A LOW PROFILE
PLACE

Good, well-composed classic dishes with a modern touch.

L'Entrecote et Les Dames

€€ VAN BAERLESTRAAT 49
80 1071 AP, OUD-ZUID
T 679 88 88 / F 470 90 20
WWW.ENTRECOTE-ET-
LES-DAMES.NL

OPEN MON-SAT 5.30-
11 PM, CLOSED SUN
RESERVATION REC.: 7-10
PERS.
SEATING: 85
GROUPS: MAX. 10
MUSIC:
FRENCH/JAZZ/LOUNGE

AMBIENCE: MODERN, IN
BETWEEN LONDON AND
PARIS

An old, but proven formula: salad, entrecôte or sole, desserts.

Entresol

€€ GELDERSEKADE 29
81 1011 EJ, CENTRUM
T 623 79 12
WWW.ENTRESOL.NU

OPEN 6-10 PM,
CLOSED MON & TUE
RESERVATION REC.
SEATING: 30
GROUPS: MAX. 30
AIRCONDITIONING

MUSIC: BACKGROUND
AMBIENCE: WELL-KEPT

A small but personal restaurant serving fine French food.

FLO Amsterdam

€€ AMSTELSTRAAT 9 (REM-
82 BRANDTPLEIN)
1017 DA, CENTRUM
T 890 47 57 / F 890 47 50
WWW.
FLOAMSTERDAM.COM

OPEN LUNCH 12 NOON-
3 PM, DINNER 5.30-11 PM,
SAT-SUN NO LUNCH
RESERVATION REC.
SEATING: 122
GROUPS: MAX. 20
BAR
AIRCONDITIONING

NO-SMOKING AREA
DOGS: PREFERABLY NOT
MOORING OPPOSITE
AMSTEL 144
NO MUSIC
AMBIENCE: ART NOUVEAU

A clone of the famous Parisian chain including La Coupole, Terminus etc

Le Garage

€€ RUYSDAELSTRAAT 54-56
83 1071 XE, OUD-ZUID
T 679 71 76 / F 662 22 49
WWW.RESTAURANT
LEGARAGE.NL

OPEN 6-11 PM,
LUNCH MON-FRI 12
NOON-2 PM
RESERVATION REC.
SEATING: 83
GROUPS: MAX. 8
BAR

AIRCONDITIONING
PRIVATE DINING ROOM
FOR 75
CATERING
VALET PARKING
MUSIC: JAZZ-CLASSICAL
AMBIENCE: MODERN

The place to see and be seen.

* Jean-Jean

€€ EERSTE ANJELIERS-
84 DWARSSTRAAT 14
1015 NR, CENTRUM
T 627 71 53
WWW.JEAN-JEAN.NL
OPEN 6-10 PM,

CLOSED MON
RESERVATION REC.
SEATING: 42
GROUPS: MAX. 14
TERRACE
DOGS: ASK FIRST
MUSIC: JAZZY, BACK-
GROUND

AMBIENCE: SIMPLE CHIC

A simple restaurant, striving to be at the top.

* De Kersentuin

€€ **INTERNATIONAL – FRENCH**
85 BILDERBERG GARDEN
HOTEL
DIJSSELHOFPLANTSOEN 7
1077 BJ, OUD-ZUID
T 570 50 00 / F 570 56 54
WWW.GARDENHOTEL.NL

OPEN LUNCH MON-FRI
12 NOON-2 PM, DINNER
MON-SAT 6-10 PM,
CLOSED SUN
RESERVATION REC.
SEATING: 100
GROUPS: MAX. 130
PRIVATE DINING ROOMS
BAR

TERRACE
MOORING AT 492 FEET
AIRCONDITIONING
VALET PARKING
MUSIC: JAZZ
AMBIENCE: FRENCH-
INFORMAL

A brasserie for the posh part of town.

** Brasserie Pays Bas

€€ GUSTAV MAHLERPLEIN 14
86 1082 MA, ZUIDERAMSTEL
T 642 06 73 / F 642 22 27
WWW.
BRASSERIEPAYSBAS.NL

OPEN MON-FRI 12 NOON-
10 PM, SAT 6-10 PM,
CLOSED SUN
RESERVATION REC. AT
WEEKENDS
SEATING: 100
GROUPS: MAX. 30
TERRACE

AIRCONDITIONING
CATERING
MUSIC: JAZZY LOUNGE
AMBIENCE: MODERN AND
COMFORTABLE

A classical brasserie in a modern place – just very good.

Pont 13

€ STAVANGERWEG 891
87 1013 AX, WESTERPARK
W 770 27 22
WWW.PONT13.NL

OPEN FROM 6 PM; SUN
FROM 12 NOON,
CLOSED MON
RESERVATION REC.
SEATING: 85
GROUPS: MAX 10
BAR
TERRACE: ON DECK

PRIVATE DINING ROOM:
THE FLIGHT-DECK, MAX 8
MOORING
TAKEAWAY POSSIBLE
MUSIC: QUIET WORLDMU-
SIC LATE AT NIGHT
AMBIENCE: LOW TECH

A little rough around the edges (an old ferry) but good, unpretentious food.

Le Relais

€ IN HOTEL DE L'EUROPE
88 NIEUWE DOELEN-
STRAAT 2-8
1012 CP, CENTRUM
T 531 17 04 / F 531 17 78
WWW.LEUROPE.NL

OPEN DAILY 12 NOON-
11 PM
RESERVATION REC.
SEATING: 28
GROUPS: MAX. 16
TERRACE
MOORING

MUSIC: BACKGROUND
AMBIENCE: CLASSIC

The brasserie department of one of the finest restaurants of Amsterdam, Excelsior. Same cuisine.

Café Roux

€€ OUDEZIJDS VOORBURG-
89 WAL 197
1012 EX, CENTRUM
T 555 35 60 / F 555 32 90
WWW.THEGRAND.NL

OPEN LUNCH 12 NOON-
2.30 PM, DINNER 6.30-
10.30 PM
RESERVATION REC.
NUMBER OF SEAT: 80
GROUPS: MAX. 16
BAR

TERRACE
NO DOGS
MOORING
AIRCONDITIONING
MUSIC: CLASSICAL-JAZZ
AMBIENCE: MODERN-
ART DECO

Well-prepared French food under the supervision of Albert Roux.

Café Schiller

€ REMBRANDTPLEIN 26
90 1017 CV, CENTRUM
T 624 98 46
F 624 89 64
WWW.VRIENDENVAN-
SCHILLER.NL

OPEN DAILY 4-10 PM,
4-8 PM 'DISH OF THE DAY'
€ 10 ('SIMPLE DUTCH
FARE')
SEATING: 55
BAR
TERRACE
NO CREDITCARDS

NO-SMOKING AREA
CATERING IN SUMMER
MUSIC: OLD-FASHIONED
AMBIENCE: CLASSICAL
POSH PUB

More than excellent pub-food – or is it an old fashioned restaurant after all? Not to be confused with Brasserie Schiller next door.

Van de kaart

€€ PRINSENGRACHT 512
91 1017 KH, CENTRUM
T 625 92 32
WWW.VANDEKAART.COM

OPEN 6.30-10.30 PM,
CLOSED SUN
RESERVATION REC.
SEATING: 34 + 4 AT THE
CHEF'S TABLE
GROUPS: MAX. 34

NO DOGS
MUSIC: MIXED
AMBIENCE: MODERN

Small, modern restaurant.

** VandeMarkt

€€ SCHOLLENBRUG-
92 STRAAT 8-9
1091 EZ, OOST/
WATERGRAAFSMEER
T 468 69 58 / F 463 04 54

WWW.VANDEMARKT.NL
OPEN TUE-SAT 6-10 PM,
CLOSED SUN & MON, EX-
CEPT ON REQUEST
SEATING: 56
GROUPS: MAX. 60
BAR

TERRACE
NO DOGS
CATERING
NO MUSIC
AMBIENCE: MODERN

Well-designed modern place with good food.

FRENCH — TOP OF THE RANGE

*** Beddington's

€€€ UTRECHTSEDWARS-
93 STRAAT 141
1017 WE, CENTRUM
T 620 73 93

OPEN 7-10.30 PM,
CLOSED SUN & MON
RESERVATION REC.
SEATING: 24
GROUPS: MAX. 7

NO DOGS
NO MUSIC
AMBIENCE: SIMPLE AND
STYLISH

Small place with very personal variety of French/English/Japanese fusion, with a female touch.

* Blauw aan de wal

€€ OUDEZIJDS ACHTER-
94 BURGWAL 99
1012 DD, CENTRUM
T 330 22 57 / F 330 20 06

OPEN 6.30-11.30 PM,
CLOSED SUN
RESERVATION REC.
SEATING: 55
GROUPS: MAX. 12
AIRCONDITIONING
NO-SMOKING AREA

NO DOGS
NO MUSIC
AMBIENCE: MODERN,
WELL-KEPT

A stylish oasis in the red light district with well-prepared French food.

*** Bordewijk

€€€ NOORDERMARKT 7
95 1015 MV, CENTRUM
T 624 38 99 / F 420 66 03

OPEN 7-10.30 PM,
CLOSED MON
RESERVATION REC.
SEATING: 45
MUSIC: NONE OR

CLASSICAL
AMBIENCE: MODERN

My personal favourite with simple, modern surroundings and luscious Mediterranean food.

** Het Bosch

€€€ JOLLENPAD 10
96 1081 KC, ZUIDERAMSTEL
T 644 58 00 / F 644 19 64
WWW.HETBOSCH.COM

OPEN 12 NOON-2 PM &
6-9 PM,
CLOSED SAT & SUN
RESERVATION REC.
SEATING: 35
GROUPS: MAX. 55

BAR
TERRACE
MOORING
NO DOGS
NO MUSIC
AMBIENCE: CLASSIC

Outside of everything, boarding a lake, with excellent French cuisine.

*** Christophe'

€€€ LELIEGRACHT 46
97 1015 DH, CENTRUM
T 625 08 07 / F 638 91 32
WWW.CHRISTOPHE.NL

OPEN 6.30-10.30 PM,
CLOSED SUN & MON,
LUNCH FROM 20 PERS.
ON APPOINTMENT
RESERVATION REC.
SEATING: 50
GROUPS: MAX. 70

PRIVATE DINING ROOM:
MAX. 14
BAR
AIRCONDITIONING
NO MUSIC
AIRCONDITIONING: MO-
DERN-CLASSIC

Fancy fine food in Michelin starred restaurant. Recently taken over by chef Jean-Joel.

* Ciel Bleu

€€€ OKURA HOTEL
98 FERD. BOLSTRAAT 333
1072 LH, OUD-ZUID
T 678 74 50 / F 671 23 44
WWW.OKURA.NL

OPEN DAILY
6.30-10.30 PM
RESERVATION REC.
SEATING: 80
GROUPS: MAX. 24 (IN
STARLIGHT-ROOM MAX.
60)
PRIVATE DINING ROOMS

BAR
NO DOGS
MOORING
AIRCONDITIONING
MUSIC: MUZAK
AMBIENCE: CLASSIC-RO-
MANTIC

Haute cuisine in the highest restaurant (23rd floor) for a high price.

** Excelsior

€€€ IN HOTEL DE L'EUROPE
99 NIEUWE DOELEN-
STRAAT 2-8
1012 CP, CENTRUM
T 531 17 05 / F 531 17 78
WWW.LEUROPE.NL

OPEN 12.30 PM-2.30 PM,
7-10.30 PM, IN WINTER
NO LUNCH AT SAT & SUN
RESERVATION REC.
SEATING: 100
GROUPS: MAX. 180
THEATREMENU 6 PM-11 PM
PRIVATE DINING ROOMS
BAR

TERRACE
MOORING
DRESSCODE
AIRCONDITIONING
CATERING
VALET PARKING
MUSIC: LIVE PIANO
AMBIENCE: CLASSIC

Excellent restaurant, both classical and modern, with French chef. Nice riverside terrace in summer.

** De Groene Lanteerne

€€ HAARLEMMERSTRAAT 43
100 1013 EJ, CENTRUM
T 624 19 52

OPEN 7-11 PM,
CLOSED SUN & HOLIDAYS
RESERVATION REC.
AIRCONDITIONING
SEATING: 36
GROUPS: MAX. 20

CASH PAYMENT ONLY
MUSIC: CLASSICAL
AMBIENCE: ROMANTIC -
OLD-DUTCH

Small French restaurant with great winelist.

* Halvemaan

€€€ VAN LEIJENBERGH-
101 LAAN 320
1082 DD, ZUIDERAMSTEL
T 644 03 48; 0800-022 44 77
(RESERVATION REC.);
F 644 17 77
WWW.HALVEMAAN.NL

OPEN FOR LUNCH 12
NOON-2.30 PM, DINNER
6.30-10.30 PM,
CLOSED SAT & SUN
RESERVATION REC.
SEATING: 50
GROUPS: MAX. 50
PRIVATE DINING ROOM:
MAX. 20

TERRACE
DOGS: ASK FIRST
NO MUSIC
AMBIENCE: MODERN

Famous Dutch innovator chef, nicely situated restaurant that was built for him.

** De Kas

€€ PARK FRANKENDAEL
102 KAMERLINGH
ONNESLAAN 3
1097 DE, OOST/
WATERGRAAFSMEER
T 462 45 62 / F 462 45 63
WWW.RESTAURANTDEKAS.NL

OPEN 12 NOON-2 PM &
6-10 PM,
SAT DINNER ONLY,
CLOSED SUN
RESERVATION REC.
SEATING: 100
GROUPS: MAX. 150
BAR
TERRACE

PRIVATE DINING ROOMS:
MAX. 70
AIRCONDITIONING
NO DOGS
NO MUSIC
AMBIENCE: MODERN-
COMFORTABLE

Fantastic greenhouse restaurant serves its own organically grown produce in fixed menu.

*** La Rive

€€€ AMSTEL HOTEL
103 PROF. TULPPLEIN 1
1018 GX, CENTRUM
T 520 32 64 / F 520 32 66
WWW.
RESTAURANTLARIVE.COM

OPEN
LUNCH MON-FRI 12
NOON-2 PM,
DINNER MON-SAT 6.30-
10.30 PM, CLOSED SUN
RESERVATION REC.
SEATING: 65
GROUPS: MAX. 16
PRIVATE DINING ROOMS
IN WINE-CELLAR
BAR

TERRACE
NO DOGS
MOORING
DRESSCODE
AIRCONDITIONING
CHEF'S TABLE (6)
CATERING
VALET PARKING
MUSIC: CLASSICAL
AMBIENCE: CLASSIC-RO-
MANTIC-INTERNATIONAL

Fanciest place in Amsterdam, excellent food, excellent wines, excellent, not too formal service.

Rosarium

€€€ AMSTELPARK 1
104 (EUROPABOULEVARD)
1083 HZ, ZUIDERAMSTEL
T 644 40 85 / F 646 60 04
WWW.ROSARIUM.NET

OPEN LUNCH 12 NOON-
2.30 PM, DINNER 6-
9.30 PM,
CLOSED SAT & SUN, BUT
ON REQUEST FOR
GROUPS
RESERVATION REC.

SEATING: 50
GROUPS: MAX. 300
BAR
PRIVATE DINING ROOMS
TERRACE
MUSIC: MODERN MUZAK
AMBIENCE: LUXURIOUS

Luxurious modern restaurant in a park near RAI exhibition centre.

*** d'Theeboom

€€ SINGEL 210
105 1016 AB, CENTRUM
T 623 84 20 / F 421 25 12
WWW.THEEBOOM.COM

OPEN DAILY 6-10 PM
RESERVATION REC.
SEATING: 45
GROUPS: MAX. 70
BAR
TERRACE

MUSIC: CLASSICAL
AMBIENCE: FRENCH
BISTRO

Quiet restaurant with French owner and chef .

** Van Vlaanderen

€€ WETERINGSCHANS 175
106 1017 XD, CENTRUM
T 622 82 92

OPEN 6.30-10.30 PM,
FRI & SAT 7 PM,
CLOSED SUN & MON
RESERVATION REC.
SEATING: 45

GROUPS: MAX. 22
TERRACE
MOORING
MUSIC: JAZZ-FRENCH
AMBIENCE: MODERN

Nice modern French restaurant, not too posh.

Zuid Zeeland

€€ **EUROPEAN**
107 HERENGRACHT 413
1017 BP, CENTRUM
T 624 31 54 / F 428 31 71
WWW.ZUIDZEELAND.NL

OPEN LUNCH
MON-FRI 12 NOON-
2.30 PM,
DINNER DAILY 6-11 PM
RESERVATION REC.
SEATING: 45
GROUPS: MAX. 20

TERRACE
CATERING
MUSIC: CLASSICAL/JAZZ
AMBIENCE: POST-MO-
DERN

Popular with writers and publishers.

INDONESIAN

* Blue Pepper

€€ NASSAUKADE 366
108 1054 AB, OUD-WEST
T 489 70 39
WWW.RESTAURANT
BLUEPEPPER.NL

OPEN DAILY 6-11 PM
RESERVATION REC.
SEATING: 40
GROUPS: MAX. 30
CATERING
MUSIC: LOUNGE
AMBIENCE: MODERN

Indonesian food modern style.

** Djago

€ WEST-JAVANESE
109 SCHELDEPLEIN 18
1078 GR, ZUIDERAMSTEL
T 664 20 13 / F 676 35 16

OPEN 5-9.30 PM,
CLOSED SAT
RESERVATION REC.
SEATING: 60
GROUPS: MAX. 25
BAR

TERRACE
TAKEAWAY POSSIBLE
NO MUSIC
AMBIENCE: SIMPLE

Indonesian food old style.

Indrapura

€€ SUMATRAN–JAVANESE
110 REMBRANDTPLEIN 40-42
1017 CV, CENTRUM
T 623 73 29 / F 624 90 78
WWW.INDRAPURA.NL

OPEN DAILY 5-10 PM
RESERVATION REC.
SEATING: 150
GROUPS: MAX. 150
AIRCONDITIONING
PRIVATE DINING ROOMS:
UPPER FLOOR

TERRACE: LIMITED
CATERING
MUSIC: FRI/SAT/SUN LIVE
JAZZPIANIST
AMBIENCE: MODERN-
ROMANTIC-COLONIAL
INDONESIAN

Indonesian food in colonial surroundings.

* Kadijk

€ KADIJKSPLEIN 5
111 1018 AB, CENTRUM
T 06 177 444 11
WWW.CAFEKADIJK.NL

OPEN DAILY 12 NOON-
10 PM
RESERVATION REC.: FROM
6 PERS.
SEATING: 25
GROUPS: MAX. 15
BAR
TERRACE

CASH PAYMENT ONLY
MOORING AT ENTRE-
POTDOK
MUSIC: QUIET POP AND
SOUL
AMBIENCE: VERY, VERY
SIMPLE

A small café with few tables, but with excellent Indonesian food.

Sama Sebo

€€ P.C. HOOFTSTRAAT 27
112 1071 BL, OUD-ZUID
T 662 81 46 / F 664 31 42
WWW.SAMASEBO.COM

OPEN 12 NOON-3 PM,
5-10.30 PM, CLOSED SUN
& HOLIDAYS
RESERVATION REC.
SEATING: 40
GROUPS: MAX. 20

BAR
TERRACE
AIRCONDITIONING
MUSIC: FOLKLORISTIC
AMBIENCE: FOLKLORISTIC

Traditional Indonesian pub food with back room.

Srikandi

€€ STADHOUDERSKADE 31
113 1071 ZD, OUD-ZUID
T 664 04 08 / F 669 27 10
WWW.SRIKANDI.NL

OPEN 5-10 PM
RESERVATION REC.
SEATING: 80
GROUPS: MAX. 50
BAR
PRIVATE DINING ROOMS

AIRCONDITIONING
TAKEAWAY POSSIBLE
CATERING
MUSIC: INDONESIAN
AMBIENCE: SIMPLE-
ROMANTIC

Nice, but average Indonesian restaurant.

Sukasari

€€ DAMSTRAAT 26-28
[114] 1012 JM, CENTRUM
T 624 00 92

OPEN MON-WED 5-
9.30 PM,
THU-SAT 12 NOON-
9.30 PM, CLOSED SUN
SEATING: 80

GROUPS: MAX. 50
BAR
TAKEAWAY POSSIBLE
NO MUSIC
AMBIENCE: FOLKLORISTIC

From Indonesian snackbar to restaurant, traditional.

** Tempo Doeloe

€€ UTRECHTSESTRAAT 75
[115] 1017 VJ, CENTRUM
T 625 67 18 / F 639 23 42
WWW.TEMPODOELOE
RESTAURANT.NL

OPEN 6-11.30 PM,
CLOSED SUN
RESERVATION REC.
SEATING: 48
GROUPS: MAX. 50
WHEELCHAIRS: LIMITED
BAR

AIRCONDITIONING
TAKEAWAY POSSIBLE:
LIMITED
CATERING
MUSIC: CLASSICAL-
FOLKLORISTIC
AMBIENCE: ROMANTIC

The best Indonesian restaurant in town, hot food from Sulawesi. Traditional (rijsttafel) and modern menu.

** Tujuh Maret

€ UTRECHTSESTRAAT 73
[116] 1017 VJ, CENTRUM
T 427 98 65 / F 427 66 22
WWW.TUJUH-MARET.NL

OPEN DAILY 12 NOON-
10 PM
RESERVATION REC.
SEATING: 45
GROUPS: MAX. 24
NO DOGS

TAKEAWAY POSSIBLE
CATERING
AMBIENCE: SIMPLE

Takeaway turned into restaurant, with annex.

Warung Spang-Makandra

€ **SURINAMESE-JAVANESE**
[117] GERARD DOUSTRAAT 39
1072 VK, OUD-ZUID
T 670 50 81 / F 470 85 44
WWW.SPANGMAKANDRA.NL

OPEN 11 AM-10 PM, SUN
1 PM, CLOSED MON
SEATING: 24
GROUPS: MAX. 24
CASH PAYMENT ONLY
CATERING
TAKEAWAY POSSIBLE
MUSIC: INDONESIAN

AMBIENCE: VERY SIMPLE

Takeaway with a few tables.

INTERNATIONAL

De Admiraal

€€ HERENGRACHT 319
[118] 1016 AV, CENTRUM
T 625 43 34 / F 615 16 83
WWW.DE-OOIEVAAR.NL

OPEN 4.30 PM-MIDNIGHT,
SAT 5 PM-MIDNIGHT,
CLOSED SUN
RESERVATION REC.
SEATING: 95
GROUPS: MAX. 100

PRIVATE DINING ROOMS
BAR
TERRACE
MOORING
MUSIC: JAZZ-CLASSICAL
AMBIENCE: AUTHENTIC

Seventeenth century traditional surroundings for varied food and drinks.

The Dylan

€€€ KEIZERSGRACHT 384
[119] 1016 GB, CENTRUM
T 530 20 10 / F 530 20 30
WWW.
DYLANAMSTERDAM.COM

OPEN LUNCH MON-FRI
12 NOON-2 PM, TEA MON-
SUN 3-5 PM,
DINNER MON-SAT FROM
6.30 PM,
BRUNCH SUN 12.30 PM-
2.30 PM

RESERVATION REC.
SEATING: 60
BAR
MUSIC: LOUNGE
AMBIENCE: MODERN-
CLASSIC

Fine French food with a slight touch of the Maghreb in old Dutch institution.

*The Garlic Queen

€€ REGULIERSDWARS-
120 STRAAT 27
1017 BJ, CENTRUM
T/F 422 64 26
WWW.GARLICQUEEN.NL

OPEN 6-MIDNIGHT,
FRI & SAT 6 PM-1 AM,
CLOSED MON & TUE
RESERVATION REC.
SEATING: 32
GROUPS: MAX. 5
WHEELCHAIRS: SMALL
ONES

BAR
MUSIC: CLASSICAL-
FOLKLORISTIC
AMBIENCE: ROMANTIC

Modern dishes for garlic lovers.

*Gespot

€€ PRINSENGRACHT 422
121 1016 JC, CENTRUM
T 320 37 33 / F 320 60 22
WWW.RESTAURANT-
GESPOT.NL

OPEN DAILY 12 NOON-
11 PM
RESERVATION REC. AT
WEEKEND
SEATING: 74
GROUPS: MAX. 20
BAR

TERRACE
DOGS: PREFERABLY NOT
MUSIC: WORLDMUSIC
AMBIENCE: MODERN

Modern, with a Caribbean touch.

Kookpunt

€ MARCUSSTRAAT 52 B
122 1091 TK, OOST/
WATERGRAAFSMEER
T 463 23 99

OPEN TUE-SUN 3 PM-
MIDNIGHT, LUNCH ON
REQUEST FROM 10 PERS.
SEATING: 60
GROUPS: MAX. 45
BAR

TERRACE
NO CREDITCARDS
NO-SMOKING AREA
MUSIC: SOUL/JAZZ
AMBIENCE: SIMPLE

Simple eatery for the financially challenged.

*De Kroonluchter

€€ UTRECHTSESTRAAT 141
123 1017 VM, CENTRUM
T 428 1074 / F 428 3481
WWW.RESTAURANTDE-
KROONLUCHTER.NL

OPEN TUE-SAT 6-11 PM,
CLOSED SUN & MON
RESERVATION REC.
SEATING: 65
GROUPS: MAX. 15
BAR
TERRACE

MUSIC: JAZZY
AMBIENCE: POST
MODERN

Fine food in relaxed surroundings.

*Lof

€€ HAARLEMMERSTRAAT 62
124 1013 ES, CENTRUM
T 620 29 97

OPEN 7-11 PM,
CLOSED MON
RESERVATION REC.
SEATING: 55
GROUPS: MAX. 20
PRIVATE DINING ROOMS

ENTRESOL
AIRCONDITIONING
CATERING
NO MUSIC
AMBIENCE: SIMPLE

Here they re-invent the wheel every day.

*The Movies Wild Kitchen

€ HAARLEMMERDIJK 159
25 1013 KH, CENTRUM
T 626 70 69 / F 620 67 58
WWW.THEMOVIES.NL

OPEN DAILY 5.30-
10.30 PM
RESERVATION REC.
SEATING: 50
GROUPS: MAX. 20
BAR
NO-SMOKING AREA

MUSIC: WORLDMUSIC
AMBIENCE: CLASSIC
BISTRO

A classical simple theatre-restaurant.

* Puyck

€€ **FUSION**
126 CEINTUURBAAN 147
1072 GB, OUD-ZUID
T 676 76 77 / F 676 76 76
WWW.PUYCK.NL

OPEN 5.30-10.30 PM,
CLOSED SUN
RESERVATION REC.
SEATING: 60
GROUPS: MAX. 14
AIRCONDITIONING
MUSIC: ONLY IN THE

EARLY EVENING
AMBIENCE: MODERN

Where fusion does not yet become confusion.

ITALIAN

** Angoletto

€€ HEMONYSTRAAT 18
127 1074 BP, OUD-ZUID
T/F 676 41 82

OPEN 6-11.30 PM,
CLOSED SAT
RESERVATION REC. FROM
6 PERS.
SEATING: 35
GROUPS: MAX. 15
CREDITCARDS:

(VISA > €75)
TERRACE
NO DOGS
TAKEAWAY POSSIBLE
NO MUSIC
AMBIENCE: SIMPLE

Pizzeria turned restaurant; simple, authentic, good quality.

** Bellini

€€ NEDERHOVEN 17
128 1083 AM, ZUIDERAMSTEL
T 644 83 90 / F 543 64 57

OPEN LUNCH MON-FRI
12 NOON-3 PM, DINNER
DAILY 5-11 PM
RESERVATION REC.
SEATING: 56
GROUPS: MAX. 60
TERRACE
AIRCONDITIONING

PRIVATE DINING ROOMS:
SUN LOUNGE
DOGS: PREFERABLY NOT
TAKEAWAY POSSIBLE
CATERING
MUSIC: ITALIAN
AMBIENCE: COSY

Fancy oldfashioned, with excellent specialities.

* Ristorante Bice

€€€ STADHOUDERSKADE 7-9
129 1054 ES, OUD-WEST
T 589 88 70
WWW.BICE.NL

OPEN DINNER 6.30-10.30
PM, CLOSED SUN, LUNCH
ONLY ON REQUEST
RESERVATION REC.
SEATING: 85
GROUPS: MAX. 40
BAR

NO DOGS
MOORING
AIRCONDITIONING
MUSIC: CLASSICAL-
ITALIAN
AMBIENCE: MODERN-
TRENDY

Where you wear Armani and have a pigtail.

* Ristorante Caruso

€€€ SINGEL 550
130 1017 AZ, CENTRUM
T 623 83 20 / F 626 61 83
WWW.
JOLLYHOTELS.NL/DINING

OPEN DAILY 6.30-10 PM
RESERVATION REC.
SEATING: 120
GROUPS: MAX. 50
PRIVATE DINING ROOMS
AIRCONDITIONING
NO DOGS
MUSIC: CLASSICAL

AMBIENCE: CLASSIC-
MEDITERRANEAN

Huge stylish and fancy Italian restaurant. If you're lucky, there is no live music.

* Da Damiano

€ JAN PIETER HEIJE-
131 STRAAT 139
1054 MG, OUD-WEST
T 685 07 95

OPEN 5-11 PM,
CLOSED MON
RESERVATION REC.
SEATING: 70
GROUPS: MAX. 30
TERRACE

TAKEAWAY POSSIBLE
CASH PAYMENT ONLY
MUSIC: ITALIAN MUZAK
AMBIENCE: SIMPLE

Very simple, but with a real Italian heart.

104

Da Noi

€€ HAARLEMMERDIJK 128
132 1013 JJ, CENTRUM
T 620 14 09

OPEN 7.30 PM-MIDNIGHT,
FRI & SAT UNTIL 1 AM,
CLOSED MON
RESERVATION REC.
SEATING: 45

GROUPS: MAX. 45
PRIVATE DINING ROOMS:
MAX. 25
MUSIC: JAZZ-POP-ITALIAN
AMBIENCE: ITALIAN

Slightly fancy and fickle, but if you're lucky, very good.

* La Favola

€€ AMSTELVEENSEWEG 141-
133 143
1075 VZ, OUD-ZUID
T/F 679 66 41
WWW.RISTORANTE
LAFAVOLA.NL

OPEN 5-10.30 PM,
CLOSED MON
RESERVATION REC.
SEATING: 45
GROUPS: MAX. 40
TERRACE
AIRCONDITIONING
NO CREDITCARDS

DOGS: PREFERABLY NOT
MUSIC: ITALIAN
AMBIENCE: LIVINGROOM

A real mama-papa place, where the whole family gives a hand.

* Felicita

€ WETERINGSCHANS 187 C
134 1017 XE, CENTRUM
T/F 422 10 88
WWW.FELICITA.NL

OPEN 6-11 PM,
CLOSED MON
RESERVATION REC.
SEATING: 70
GROUPS: MAX. 70
PRIVATE DINING ROOMS

NO-SMOKING AREA
NO DOGS
CATERING
MUSIC: ITALIAN
AMBIENCE: WELL-KEPT

Here the cook is the boss, and you shall know it!

Hostaria

€ TWEEDE EGELANTIERS-
135 DWARSSTRAAT 9
1015 SB, CENTRUM
T 626 00 28

OPEN 7-10 PM,
CLOSED MON
RESERVATION REC.
SEATING: 34
GROUPS: MAX. 12
NO CREDITCARDS

NO MUSIC
AMBIENCE: SIMPLE

Small, simple and personal Italian restaurant.

** Incanto

€€ AMSTEL 2
136 1017 AA, CENTRUM
T 423 36 81/ F 423 36 82
WWW.
RESTAURANTINCANTO.NL

OPEN DAILY 11 AM-11 PM
RESERVATION REC. AT
WEEKEND
SEATING: 60
GROUPS: MAX. 18
PRIVATE DINING ROOMS
NO-SMOKING AREA

CATERING
NO MUSIC
AMBIENCE: POST
MODERN

Refined Venetian food with an unparallelled view.

* Nana Gentile

€€ NIEUWEZIJDS VOOR-
137 BURGWAL 289
1012 RL, CENTRUM
T 420 02 02 / F 427 26 67
WWW.NANAGENTILE.NL

OPEN TUE-SUN 6-10 PM,
CLOSED MON
SEATING: 34
GROUPS: MAX. 8
NO DOGS
MUSIC: BACKGROUND
AMBIENCE: MODERN

Creative modern Italian in a nice atmosphere.

La Nuova Vita

€€ WILLEMSPARKWEG 155
138 1071 GX, OUD-ZUID
T/F 679 38 68

OPEN 6-10.30 PM,
CLOSED MON
RESERVATION REC.
SEATING: 32
GROUPS: MAX. 38

AIRCONDITIONING
NO MUSIC
AMBIENCE: MODERN-
CLASSIC

Slightly formal, a little bourgeois.

* Palladio

€€ ELANDSGRACHT 64
139 1016 TX, CENTRUM
T 627 74 42
WWW.
RESTAURANTPALLADIO.NL

OPEN 6-11 PM,
CLOSED MON
RESERVATION REC.
SEATING: 50
GROUPS: MAX. 30
TERRACE: PATIO
AIRCONDITIONING

PRIVATE DINING ROOMS
MUSIC: ITALIAN, JAZZ
AMBIENCE: A SIMPLE
TRATTORIA

They have a Venetian cook now; it is better than it used to be.

** Panini

€ VIJZELGRACHT 3-5
140 1017 HM, CENTRUM
T 626 49 39 / F 330 71 22
WWW.
RESTAURANTPANINI.NL

OPEN MON-SAT 11 AM-
10 PM, SUN 12 NOON-
10 PM
RESERVATION REC.
SEATING: 50
GROUPS: MAX. 8
BAR

TERRACE
TAKEAWAY POSSIBLE
LUNCH
MUSIC: USUALLY NONE
AMBIENCE: MODERN

A small restaurant/espresso bar with a small but good menu. They bake their own bread.

Pasta e Basta

€€ NIEUWE SPIEGELSTRAAT 8
141 1017 DE, CENTRUM
T 422 22 22 / F 422 22 31
WWW.PASTAEBASTA.NL

OPEN DAILY 6-10.30 PM
RESERVATION: NECESSARY
SEATING: 112
GROUPS: MAX. 112
BAR
MOORING AT THE HEREN-

GRACHT OR KEIZERS-
GRACHT
AIRCONDITIONING
MUSIC: CLASSICAL-
OPERA-LIVE
AMBIENCE: ROMANTIC

Where the waiters sing operas and the whole restaurant swings.

Roberto's

€€ IN AMSTERDAM HILTON
142 HOTEL
APOLLOLAAN 138
1077 BG, OUD-ZUID
T 710 60 25 / F 710 60 80
WWW.
HILTONAMSTERDAM.COM

OPEN LUNCH 12 NOON-
2.30 PM, DINNER 6.30-
10.30 PM
RESERVATION: NECESSARY
SEATING: 110 INSIDE/60
OUTSIDE
GROUPS: MAX. 50
PRIVATE DINING ROOMS
BAR

TERRACE WITH WIFI
NO DOGS
MOORING
AIRCONDITIONING
MUSIC: CLASSICAL-
ITALIAN
AMBIENCE: MEDITER-
RANEAN

The Hilton Hotel version of Italian cuisine.

*** Segugio

€€ UTRECHTSESTRAAT 96
143 1017 VS, CENTRUM
T 330 15 03 / F 330 15 16
WWW.SEGUGIO.NL

OPEN 6-10 PM,
CLOSED SUN
RESERVATION REC.
SEATING: 36
GROUPS: MAX. 10
NO MUSIC

AMBIENCE: MODERN

One of the better modern Italian restaurants.

* Lo Stivale d'Oro

€ AMSTELSTRAAT 49
144 1017 DA, CENTRUM
T 638 73 07 / F 770 1177
WWW.
LOSTIVALEDORO.COM

OPEN WED-MON 5-11 PM,
CLOSED TUE
RESERVATION REC. FROM
5 PERS.
SEATING: 40
GROUPS: MAX. 8
AIRCONDITIONING

TAKEAWAY POSSIBLE
CATERING
NO MUSIC
AMBIENCE: INFORMAL
TRATTORIA

Very informal, an o sole mio restaurant.

* La Storia della Vita

€€ WETERINGSCHANS 171
145 1017 XD, CENTRUM
T/F 623 42 51
WWW.
LASTORIADELLAVITA.NL

OPEN 6.30-11 PM,
CLOSED SUN
RESERVATION REC.
SEATING: 65
GROUPS: MAX. 75
BAR
TERRACE
MUSIC: LIVE

AMBIENCE: EASY-GOING,
TRADITIONAL

You eat what the excellent cook prepares. No menu.

** A Tavola

€€ KADIJKSPLEIN 9
146 1018 AC, CENTRUM
T 625 49 94

OPEN DAILY 6-10.30 PM
RESERVATION REC.
SEATING: 45
GROUPS: FROM 8, ONLY
MENU
TERRACE

NO DOGS
CATERING
NO CREDITCARDS
NO MUSIC
AMBIENCE: VERY SIMPLE

Busy, noisy and authentic Italian.

Teatro

€ KADIJKSPLEIN 16
147 1018 AC, CENTRUM
T 623 63 13
WWW.TEATRO.NL

OPEN 5.30-11 PM,
CLOSED SUN
RESERVATION REC.
SEATING: 115
GROUPS: MAX. 50
BAR

PRIVATE DINING ROOMS
MOORING
MUSIC: ITALIAN
AMBIENCE: FOLKLORISTIC

Nice.

*** Toscanini

€€ LINDENGRACHT 75
148 1015 KD, CENTRUM
T 623 28 13
WWW.TOSCANINI.NU

OPEN 6-10.30 PM,
CLOSED SUN
RESERVATION REC.
SEATING: 70
GROUPS: MAX. 14, ONLY
MON-WED

BAR
TERRACE: SMALL, AT THE
STREETSIDE + PORCH
NO MUSIC
AMBIENCE: SIMPLE

Excellent food, nice ambience, arguably the best authentic Italian in town.

** Yam Yam Trattoria- Pizzeria

€ FREDERIK HENDRIK-
149 STRAAT 88-90
1052 HZ, OUD-WEST
T 681 50 97
WWW.YAMYAM.NL

OPEN 6-10 PM,
CLOSED MON
RESERVATION REC.
SEATING: 57
TERRACE
MUSIC: MIXED
AMBIENCE: SIMPLE-
MODERN

Simple trattoria/pizzeria. Value for money.

JAPANESE

Japanese Pancake World

€€
150 TWEEDE EGELANTIERS-
DWARSSTRAAT 24 A
1015 SC, CENTRUM
T/F 320 44 47
WWW.JAPANESE
PANCAKEWORLD.COM

OPEN DAILY 12 NOON-
10 PM
SEATING: 26
GROUPS: MAX. 6
TERRACE: SMALL
CREDITCARDS: ONLY AM.
EXPRESS
NO-SMOKING AREA AT
TEPPAN

MUSIC: JAPANESE
AMBIENCE: MODERN

Japanese fastfood for eaters with patience.

* Kagetsu

€€ HARTENSTRAAT 17
151 1016 BZ, CENTRUM
T/F 427 38 28
WWW.KAGETSU.NL

OPEN DAILY 5-11 PM
RESERVATION REC.
SEATING: 30
GROUPS: MAX. 20
CASH PAYMENT ONLY
NO SMOKING

NO DOGS
TAKEAWAY POSSIBLE
CATERING
MUSIC: JAPANESE
AMBIENCE: SIMPLE

Japanese restaurant with Japanese cooks (becoming rare).

Morita-Ya

€ ZEEDIJK 18
152 1012 AZ, CENTRUM
T 638 07 56 / F 638 85 88

OPEN 6-10 PM,
CLOSED MON
RESERVATION REC.
SEATING: 24
BAR

NO DOGS
MUSIC: JAPANESE
AMBIENCE: SIMPLE

Japanese mama cooks for you.

Shinto

€ GOVERT FLINCK-
153 STRAAT 153
1073 BS, OUD-ZUID
T 670 46 90 / F 672 77 69

OPEN DAILY 4-10 PM
SEATING: 22
GROUPS: MAX. 22
NO CREDITCARDS
TAKEAWAY POSSIBLE
CATERING

MUSIC: BACKGROUND
AMBIENCE: SIMPLE

Simple, very simple.

Teppan Yaki Hosokawa

€€€ MAX EUWEPLEIN 22
154 1017 MB, CENTRUM
T 638 80 86 / F 638 22 19
WWW.HOSOKAWA.NL

OPEN LUNCH MON-SAT
12 NOON-3 PM, DINNER
MON-SUN 5-10 PM
SUSHI-BAR
RESERVATION REC.
SEATING: 80
GROUPS: MAX. 85

PRIVATE DINING ROOMS
NO DOGS
MUSIC: BACKGROUND-
JAPANESE
AMBIENCE: JAPANESE

With the whole teppan show.

Teppan Yaki Sazanka

€€€ IN OKURA HOTEL
155 FERD. BOLSTRAAT 333
1072 LF, OUD-ZUID
T 678 74 50 / F 678 77 88
WWW.OKURA.NL

OPEN DAILY 6.30-10 PM
RESERVATION REC.
SEATING: 100
GROUPS: MAX. 100
PRIVATE DINING ROOMS
NO DOGS
MOORING
AIRCONDITIONING

MUSIC: MUZAK
AMBIENCE: FOLKLORISTIC

A better teppan is apparently also possible.

* Tokyo Café

€€ SPUI 15
156 1012 WX, CENTRUM
T 489 79 18 / F 489 71 13
WWW.TOKYOCAFE.NL

OPEN DAILY 11 AM-11 PM
RESERVATION REC.
SEATING: 200
GROUPS: MAX. 60
BAR
TERRACE
AIRCONDITIONING

PRIVATE DINING ROOMS
NO DOGS
TAKEAWAY POSSIBLE
CATERING
MUSIC: JAPANESE-
LOUNGE
AMBIENCE: MODERN

Huge, for all techniques and all tastes.

*** Yamazato

€€€ IN OKURA HOTEL
157 FERD. BOLSTRAAT 333
1072 LH, OUD-ZUID
T 678 83 51 / F 678 77 88
WWW.OKURA.NL

OPEN LUNCH 12 NOON-
2 PM,
DINNER 6-9.30 PM
RESERVATION REC.
SEATING: 128
GROUPS: MAX. 40
PRIVATE DINING ROOMS

SUSHI BAR
CATERING
MUSIC: JAPANESE
AMBIENCE: MODERN-CHIC

No doubt: the best Japanese restaurant in Holland. With kaiseki dishes.

LATIN-AMERICAN

Iguazú

€ ARGENTINIAN –
158 BRAZILIAN
PRINSENGRACHT 703
1017 JV, CENTRUM
T 420 39 10

OPEN 5-11 PM,
LUNCH FRI-SUN 12 NOON-
5 PM
RESERVATION REC.
SEATING: 50
GROUPS: MAX. 25
TERRACE

MOORING ACROSS THE
CANAL
MUSIC: SOUTH-AMERICAN
AMBIENCE: MODERN

Simple, but okay.

* Riaz

€ SURINAMESE –
159 INDONESIAN – INDIAN
BILDERDIJKSTRAAT 193
1053 KS, OUD-WEST
T 683 64 53 / F 412 56 34
WWW.RIAZ.NL

OPEN 11.30 AM-9 PM, SUN
2-9 PM, CLOSED SAT
RESERVATION REC.
SEATING: 30
GROUPS: MAX. 40
AIRCONDITIONING
TAKEAWAY POSSIBLE
CATERING

CASH PAYMENT ONLY
MUSIC: MIXED
AMBIENCE: SIMPLE

Nothing fancy, but here all Surinam soccer players get their food. Also takeaway possible.

* Samba Kitchen

€ BRAZILIAN
160 CEINTUURBAAN 63
1072 EV, OUD-ZUID
T 676 05 13
WWW.SAMBAKITCHEN.NL

OPEN TUE-SUN 5-11 PM,
CLOSED MON
RESERVATION REC.
SEATING: 46
GROUPS: MAX. 50
NO CREDITCARDS
TERRACE

CATERING
MUSIC: BRASILIAN,
SOMETIMES LIVE
AMBIENCE: MODERN-
FOLKLORISTIC

Like mardi gras in Rio.

Tango

€€ ARGENTINIAN
161 WARMOESSTRAAT 49
1012 HW, CENTRUM
T 627 24 67

OPEN MON-THU 5 PM-
MIDNIGHT,
FRI-SUN 12.30 PM-
MIDNIGHT
RESERVATION REC.
SEATING: 80

GROUPS: MAX. 35
BAR
MUSIC: TANGO
AMBIENCE: BRASSERIE-
STYLE

One of the few Argentinians that is personal, not a chain.

LUNCH

Bagels & Beans

162 FERDINAND BOLSTRAAT
70
1072 LM, OUD-ZUID
T 672 16 10
WWW.BAGELSBEANS.NL

OPEN MON-FRI 8.28
AM-5.31 PM, SAT & SUN
9.31 AM-6.01 PM
SEATING: 40
BAR
TERRACE
NO CREDITCARDS

NO-SMOKING AREA
TAKEAWAY POSSIBLE
CATERING
MUSIC: CLASSICAL AND
'JAZZY'
AMBIENCE: LUNCHROOM

CHAIN STORES:

163 KEIZERSGRACHT 504, CENTRUM
164 HAARLEMMERDIJK 122, CENTRUM
165 KONINGSPLEIN 20, CENTRUM (IN BOOKSHOP SCHELTEMA)
166 WATERLOOPLEIN 2, CENTRUM
167 RAADHUISSTRAAT 18, CENTRUM
168 VAN BAERLESTRAAT 40, OUD-ZUID
169 ZEILSTRAAT 64, OUD-ZUID
170 KINKERSTRAAT 110, OUD-WEST

Good sandwiches, excellent coffee, well-run chain.

De Bakkers-winkel

171 ROELOF HARTSTRAAT 68
1071 VM, OUD-ZUID
T 662 35 94 / F 673 96 82
WWW.
DEBAKKERSWINKEL.NL

OPEN TUE-FRI 7 AM-6 PM,
SAT 7 AM-5 PM,
SUN 10 AM-4 PM
RESERVATION REC.: ONLY
GROUPS
SEATING: 35
PRIVATE DINING ROOMS
NO SMOKING

NO CREDITCARDS
TAKEAWAY POSSIBLE

172 WARMOESSTRAAT 69
1012 HX, CENTRUM
T 489 80 00 / F 489 78 78
WWW.
DEBAKKERSWINKEL.NL

OPEN TUE-FRI 8 AM-6 PM,
SAT 8 AM-5 PM,
SUN 10 AM-5 PM
RESERVATION REC.
SEATING: 90

TAKEAWAY POSSIBLE
CLASSICAL-MODERN
AMBIENCE: SIMPLE

173 REGULATEURSHUIS
WESTERPARK OPPOSITE
STADSDEELKANTOOR
WWW.
DEBAKKERSWINKEL.NL

OPEN TUE-FRI 8 AM-6 PM,
SAT 8 AM-5 PM, SUN 10
AM-5 PM
SEATING: 70
TAKEAWAY POSSIBLE

MUSIC: CLASSICAL-
WORLDMUSIC

To eat or take away

't Blaauw Hooft

174 HENDRIK JONKERPLEIN 1
1013 KM, CENTRUM
T 623 87 21
WWW.BLAAUWHOOFT.NL

OPEN 12 NOON-1 AM, FRI
& SAT 12 NOON-2 AM
LUNCH 12 NOON-4 PM
DINNER 6-10 PM
RESERVATION REC.
SEATING: 40

GROUPS: MAX. 20
BAR
TERRACE (40 SEATS)
MUSIC: MIXED, LIVE
MUSIC IN WINTER
AMBIENCE: INFORMAL

Pub food with good luncheon.

Brasserie 3-5-3

175 NIEUWEZIJDS VOOR-
BURGWAL 353
1012 RM, CENTRUM
T 639 23 04

OPEN 10 AM-6 PM, SUN
11.30 AM-6 PM,
CLOSED MON & TUE
SEATING: 23
TERRACE
TAKEAWAY POSSIBLE

NO CREDITCARDS
MUSIC: LIGHT-MODERN
AMBIENCE: SIMPLE

Excellent tosti's.

Brasserie De Bonneterie

176 ROKIN 140
1012 LE, CENTRUM
T 626 88 00 / F 626 87 99

OPEN 10 AM-5.30 PM,
MON OPEN AT 1 PM,
THU UNTIL 9 PM,
SUN 12-17
SEATING: 70
TERRACE AT BALCONY

TAKEAWAY POSSIBLE
NO MUSIC
AMBIENCE: CHIC

Posh, with kosher specialities.

Brasserie Van Baerle

74 VAN BAERLESTRAAT 158
1071 BG, OUD-ZUID
T 679 15 32 / F 671 71 96
WWW.
BRASSERIEVANBAERLE.NL

OPEN MON-FRI 12 NOON-
11 PM, SUN 10 AM-11 PM,
SAT ONLY DINNER
RESERVATION REC.
SEATING: 50
GROUPS: MAX. 42
PRIVATE DINING ROOMS
TERRACE: GARDEN

MUSIC: JAZZ-CLASSICAL
AMBIENCE: CLASSIC

For lavish lunches. Nice garden terrace.

Caffé et Panini Esclusivi

177 AMSTELVEENSEWEG 85
1075 VW, OUD-ZUID
T/F 364 14 31

OPEN MON-FRI 8.30 AM,-
2.30 PM, SAT 10 AM-2.30
PM, CLOSED SUN
RESERVATION REC.: ONLY
BETWEEN 12-2 PM
SEATING: 45
GROUPS: MAX. 20

BAR
AIRCONDITIONING
NO CREDITCARDS
TAKEAWAY POSSIBLE
CATERING
MUSIC: POPULAR RADIO
AMBIENCE: SIMPLE

Italian sandwichshop.

Cobra

178 MUSEUMPLEIN
HOBBEMASTRAAT 18
1071 ZB, OUD-ZUID
T 470 01 11 / F 470 01 14
WWW.COBRACAFE.NL

OPEN DAILY 10 AM-8 PM
SEATING: 65
GROUPS: MAX. 70
BAR
TERRACE
AIRCONDITIONING
MUSIC: POP & JAZZ

AMBIENCE: MODERN
DESIGN

Nicely located place with good terrace. Fanciest toilets in town.

Coffee & Jazz

179 UTRECHTSESTRAAT 113
1017 VL, CENTRUM
T 624 58 51

OPEN 10.30 AM-11 PM,
CLOSED SAT-MON
SEATING: 20
MUSIC: JAZZ
AMBIENCE: SIMPLE

Indonesian lunches and fruitmixes. Small but nice.

Coffee Connection

180 NIEUWEZIJDS KOLK 33
1012 PV, CENTRUM
T/F 421 88 88

OPEN MON-SAT 8 AM-6
PM, SUN 8.30 AM-7 PM
SEATING: 35
TERRACE
PRIVATE DINING ROOMS
UPSTAIRS

NO SMOKING
TAKEAWAY POSSIBLE
CASH PAYMENT ONLY
MUSIC: JAZZ
AMBIENCE: VERY SIMPLE

Small place for Americans.

Le Delizie

181 **ITALIAN**
VIJZELGRACHT 17
1017 HM, CENTRUM
T 622 68 71
WWW.LEDELIZIE.NL

OPEN 10 AM-11 PM, SUN
11 AM-11 PM
SEATING: 28
GROUPS: MAX. 10
TAKEAWAY POSSIBLE
CATERING
MUSIC: ITALIAN

AMBIENCE: MODERN-
SIMPLE

A takeaway with a few tables. Very Italian.

Divertimento

182 SINGEL 480
1017 AW, CENTRUM
T 622 96 90

OPEN 8.30 AM-5.30 PM,
SAT UNTIL 6 PM, SUN
OPEN AT 10 AM
SEATING: 50
BAR
TERRACE
NO-SMOKING AREA AT
THE BAR

TAKEAWAY POSSIBLE
CASH PAYMENT ONLY
CATERING
MUSIC: UNTIL 12 NOON
CLASSICAL, THEN JAZZ
AMBIENCE: SIMPLE,
COMFORTABLE

Nice sandwiches with view of the flower market.

Van Dobben

183 KORTE REGULIERS-
DWARSSTRAAT 5-9
1071 BH, CENTRUM
T 624 42 00 / F 623 85 93
WWW.VANDOBBEN.COM

OPEN MON-THU 9.30 AM-
1 AM, FRI-SAT 9.30-2 AM,
SUN 11.30-8 PM
SEATING: 32
AIRCONDITIONING
BAR
CASH PAYMENT ONLY

TAKEAWAY POSSIBLE
CATERING
MUSIC: BACKGROUND
AMBIENCE: KITCHEN

Classical Dutch sandwich shop, with famous croquettes.

Lunchroom/ snackbar Dolores

184 NIEUWEZIJDS VOOR-
BURGWAL
FACING NR. 289
1012 RL, CENTRUM
T 620 33 02

OPEN 11 AM-6 PM, THU
UNTIL 9.30 PM, SUN 12
NOON-6 PM
SEATING: 7 (INSIDE)
TERRACE (20 SEATS)
CASH PAYMENT ONLY
TAKEAWAY POSSIBLE
MUSIC: BACKGROUND
AMBIENCE: MODERN,

SIMPLE

Organic snacks in minute building in the middle of the road.

Festina Lente

185 LOOIERSGRACHT 40 B
1016 VS, CENTRUM
T 638 14 12 / F 320 14 42

OPEN MON 2 PM-1 AM,
TUE-THU 10.30 AM-1 AM,
FRI 10.30-3 AM, SAT 11-
3 AM, SUN 12 NOON-1 AM
SEATING: 35
BAR

TERRACE
MOORING
AIRCONDITIONING
MUSIC: MIXED-MODERN
AMBIENCE: ECLECTIC

Nice pub food in poetic surroundings.

Greenwoods

186 SINGEL 103
1012 VG, CENTRUM
T/F 623 70 71

OPEN MON-THU 9.30 AM-
6 PM, FRI-SUN 9.30 AM-
7 PM
SEATING: 26
GROUPS: MAX. 12
TERRACE
MOORING

TAKEAWAY POSSIBLE
CASH PAYMENT ONLY
CATERING
MUSIC: LOUNGE
AMBIENCE: RUSTIC

Simple English lunches and brunches.

Herengracht

187 HERENGRACHT 435
1017 BR, CENTRUM
T 616 24 82 / F 775 02 99
WWW.
DEHERENGRACHT.NL

OPEN 11 AM-11 PM,
IN SUMMER OPEN AT
10 AM
RESERVATION REC.
SEATING: 74, CHEF'S TA-
BLE 19
GROUPS: MAX. 35

BAR
TERRACE AT THE WATER-
SIDE
PRIVATE DINING ROOMS:
ENTRESOL
MUSIC: BACKGROUND
AMBIENCE: LOUNGE

Lounge restaurant, a trifle noisy.

Highlander

188 SINT JACOBSSTRAAT 8
1012 NC, CENTRUM
T/F 420 83 21

OPEN 12 NOON-1 AM,
WEEKEND 12 NOON-2 AM,
CLOSED MON
RESERVATION REC. AT
WEEKEND
SEATING: 30

GROUPS: MAX. 30
TAKEAWAY POSSIBLE
TERRACE
MUSIC: POP
AMBIENCE: FANTASY

Exotic, Scottish, with fancy sandwiches.

Koffiehuis
De Hoek

189 PRINSENGRACHT 341
1016 HK, CENTRUM
T 625 38 72

OPEN 7.30 AM-4.30 PM,
SAT 9 AM-3.30 PM,
CLOSED MON & SUN
SEATING: 50
TERRACE
CASH PAYMENT ONLY

MUSIC: RADIO
AMBIENCE: FRIENDLY

An old Dutch 'coffeehouse'. Simple but true.

Japanese
Pancake World

150 TWEEDE EGELANTIERS-
DWARSSTRAAT 24 A
1015 SC, CENTRUM
T/F 320 44 47
WWW.JAPANESE
PANCAKEWORLD.COM

OPEN DAILY 12 NOON-
10 PM
SEATING: 26
GROUPS: MAX. 6
TERRACE: SMALL
CREDITCARDS: ONLY AM.
EXPRESS
NO-SMOKING AREA AT
TEPPAN

MUSIC: JAPANESE
AMBIENCE: MODERN

Japanese fastfood for eaters with patience.

Brasserie
De Joffers

190 WILLEMSPARKWEG 163
1071 GZ, OUD-ZUID
T/F 673 03 60
WWW.DEJOFFERS.NL

OPEN 8 AM-8 PM, SAT
8 AM-6 PM,
SUN 9 AM-6 PM
SEATING: 50
TERRACE
MUSIC: CLASSICAL-JAZZ
AMBIENCE: THIRTIES

Nice sedate place for breakfast and lunches.

Kapitein Zeppos

191 GEBED ZONDER END 5
1012 HS, CENTRUM
T 624 20 57 / F 639 25 28
WWW.ZEPPOS.NL

OPEN LUNCH 11 AM-
3.30 PM, DINNER 5.30-
11 PM
SEATING: 42
GROUPS: MAX. 12
BAR

TERRACE ALSO INSIDE
UNDER OPEN ROOF
PRIVATE DINING ROOMS:
25
MUSIC: CLASSICAL-JAZZ
AMBIENCE: CAFÉ-LIKE

Busy pub with extensive food facilities. Nice patio.

Kef, De Franse Kaasmakers

192 MARNIXSTRAAT 192
1016 TJ, CENTRUM
T 420 00 97
WWW.KAASVANKEF.NL

OPEN WED-FRI 12 NOON-
8 PM, SAT 10 AM-6 PM,
SUN 12 NOON-6 PM
SEATING: 15
CATERING
NO CREDITCARDS
NO MUSIC

AMBIENCE: SIMPLE

For cheese, bread and wine. Just a few tables.

Kismet

193 TURKISH
ALBERT CUYPSTRAAT 64
1072 CW, OUD-ZUID
T 671 47 68

OPEN DAILY 8 AM-10 PM
SEATING: 16
CASH PAYMENT ONLY
TAKEAWAY POSSIBLE
CATERING
NO MUSIC

AMBIENCE: SIMPLE

Takeaway with tables. Good quality food.

Het Koffie-keldertje

194 FREDERIKSPLEIN 4
1017 XM, CENTRUM
T 626 34 24

OPEN 9 AM-4.30 PM,
CLOSED SAT & SUN
SEATING: 32
CASH PAYMENT ONLY
AIRCONDITIONING
TERRACE

TAKEAWAY POSSIBLE
NO MUSIC
AMBIENCE: COSY

A one-woman show with the best meatball and lots of personality.

't Kuyltje

195 GASTHUISMOLENSTEEG 9
1016 AM, CENTRUM
T 620 10 45 / F 620 86 66
WWW.KUYLTJE.NL

OPEN 7 AM-4 PM,
CLOSED SAT & SUN
SEATING: 12
AIRCONDITIONING
CASH PAYMENT ONLY
TAKEAWAY POSSIBLE

NO MUSIC
AMBIENCE: SIMPLE

Excellent sandwiches with meat from own farm.

Luxembourg

196 SPUI 22-24
1012 XA, CENTRUM
T 620 62 64 / F 638 51 75
WWW.LUXEMBOURG.NL

OPEN 9-1 AM, FRI & SAT
9-2 AM
SEATING: 150
GROUPS: MAX. 20
BAR
TERRACE

MUSIC: MIXED, OFTEN DJ
OR LIVE ON SUNDAY
AFTERNOON
AMBIENCE: CLASSIC

Well-frequented address for breakfast, lunch and dinner, with extensive snack menu.

Pompadour Lunchroom

[197] KERKSTRAAT 148
1017 GR, CENTRUM
T 330 09 81 / F 624 79 19
WWW.PATISSERIE
POMPADOUR.COM

OPEN MON-SAT 10 AM-
5 PM, CLOSED SUN
SEATING: 30
GROUPS: MAX. 20
NO MUSIC
AMBIENCE: MODERN

Excellent chocolaterie just opened its own tearoom.

Puccini

[198] STAALSTRAAT 21
1011 JK, CENTRUM
T 620 84 58
WWW.PUCCINI.NL

OPEN 8.30 AM-6 PM,
SAT & SUN 10 AM-6 PM,
AT EVENINGSHOWS IN
MUZIEKTHEATER UNTIL 8
PM
RESERVATION REC. ONLY
FOR DINNER

SEATING: 32
TERRACE
NO CREDITCARDS
MUSIC: SOMETIMES
CLASSICAL
AMBIENCE: MODERN-
LOUNGE

Opposite the opera: good sandwiches, good tea etc.

Sal Meijer

[199] SCHELDESTRAAT 45
1078 GG, ZUIDERAMSTEL
T 673 13 13 / F 670 45 07

OPEN 10 AM-7.30 PM, FRI
10 AM-2 PM, CLOSED SAT
SEATING: 55
TAKEAWAY POSSIBLE
NO MUSIC

AMBIENCE: SANDWICH-
SHOP

Kosher food; ask for the best fishcake in town.

Singel 404

[200] SINGEL 404
1016 AK, CENTRUM
T/F 428 01 54

OPEN 10.30 AM-7 PM
SEATING: 45
TERRACE
NO CREDITCARDS
MUSIC: CLASSICAL-JAZZ

AMBIENCE: SIMPLE

Simple eatery, terrace by the waterside.

Soup en Zo

[201] JODENBREESTRAAT 94-A
1011 NS, CENTRUM
T 422 22 43
WWW.SOUPENZO.NL

OPEN 11 AM-8 PM, SAT &
SUN 12 NOON-7 PM
SEATING: 10
TERRACE
TAKEAWAY POSSIBLE
CATERING

NO CREDITCARDS
MUSIC: MIXED
AMBIENCE: SNACKBAR

[202] NIEUWE SPIEGEL-
STRAAT 54
1017 DG, CENTRUM
T 330 77 81
WWW.SOUPENZO.NL

OPEN 11 AM-7 PM, SAT
12 NOON-6 PM,
CLOSED SUN
BAR
TAKEAWAY POSSIBLE

CATERING
NO CREDITCARDS
MUSIC: MIXED
AMBIENCE: SNACKBAR

A real soup kitchen.

Tjin's Exotische Broodjes

203 VAN WOUSTRAAT 17,
OUD-ZUID
204 BIJLMERPLEIN 527,
ZUIDOOST
205 KINKERSTRAAT 5,
OUD-WEST
206 VAN LEIJENBERGHLAAN
134, ZUIDERAMSTEL
207 PIETER CALANDLAAN 15,
SLOTERVAART / OVER-
TOOMSEVELD
WWW.TJINS.NL

OPEN USUALLY
MON-SAT 9 AM-6 PM,
CHECK WEBSITE
TAKEAWAY POSSIBLE
CASH PAYMENT ONLY
CATERING: T 673 57 71 /
F 673 57 72
MUSIC: SOUTH-AMERICAN
AMBIENCE: SANDWICH-
SHOP

Exotic sandwiches from Surinam, very professional.

Tjin's International Foodstore

208 EERSTE VAN DER HELST-
STRAAT 64
1072 NZ, OUD-ZUID
T 671 77 08 / F 664 37 30

OPEN 10 AM-8 PM,
CLOSED SUN
SEATING: 5
NO CREDITCARDS
TAKEAWAY POSSIBLE
MUSIC: RADIO
AMBIENCE: SNACKBAR

Little snackbar and takeaway with well-stocked shop.

Tokyo Café

156 JAPANESE
SPUI 15
1012 WX, CENTRUM
T 489 79 18 / F 489 71 13
WWW.TOKYOCAFE.NL

OPEN DAILY 11 AM-11 PM
RESERVATION REC.
SEATING: 200
GROUPS: MAX. 60
BAR
TERRACE
AIRCONDITIONING

PRIVATE DINING ROOMS
NO DOGS
TAKEAWAY POSSIBLE
CATERING
MUSIC: JAPANESE-
LOUNGE
AMBIENCE: MODERN

Big allround Japanese place.

B. Wouda

209 ROZENBOOMSTEEG 8
1012 PR, CENTRUM
T/F 622 30 72

OPEN 7.30 AM-5 PM,
SAT 10 AM-4.30 PM,
CLOSED SUN
TERRACE
AIRCONDITIONING
TAKEAWAY POSSIBLE

CASH PAYMENT ONLY
CATERING
MUSIC: CLASSICAL
AMBIENCE: SANDWICH-
SHOP

Small classical sandwichshop. Ask for Sandwich Johannes (pastrami/liver).

De IJsbreker

210 WEESPERZIJDE 23
1091 EC, OOST /
WATERGRAAFSMEER
T 468 18 08 / F 468 12 55
WWW.YSBREKERCAFE.NL

OPEN 9-1 AM, FRI & SAT
9-2 AM
SEATING: INSIDE 50,
OUTSIDE 100
GROUPS: MAX. 25
BAR
TERRACE

DOGS: ONLY OUTSIDE
NO CREDITCARDS
MUSIC: CLASSICAL AT
DAYTIME, JAZZ AT NIGHT
AMBIENCE: INFORMAL

Theatre restaurant with nice quiet terrace by the riverside.

Zen

211 FRANS HALSSTRAAT 38
1072 BS, CENTRUM
T 627 06 07 / F 330 59 05

OPEN 12 NOON-9 PM,
CLOSED SUN & MON
SEATING: 12
TERRACE
CASH PAYMENT ONLY

TAKEAWAY POSSIBLE
MUSIC: BACKGROUND,
JAPANESE
AMBIENCE: SIMPLE

Simple sober and personal, good Japanese food.

TRENDY

Barok

€€ WOLVENSTRAAT 22-24
212 1016 EP, CENTRUM
T 330 74 70 / F 330 75 45
WWW.
RESTAURANTBAROK.NL

OPEN MON-WED 6-10 PM,
THU-SAT 4-11 PM, SUN
4-10 PM
SEATING: 80
GROUPS: MAX. 40
AIRCONDITIONING
BAR

TERRACE
MUSIC: LOUNGE
AMBIENCE: BAROQUE

Fancy lounging, but good food.

Blender

€€ VAN DER PALMKADE 16
213 1051 RE, WESTERPARK
T 486 98 60 / F 486 98 51
WWW.BLENDER.TO

OPEN 6-10.30 PM,
FRI & SAT UNTIL 11 PM
RESERVATION REC.
SEATING: 70
GROUPS: MAX. 50
BAR

TERRACE
MUSIC: LOUNGE
AMBIENCE: MODERN

Like a nightclub, with music after 9 pm, but good food.

Bond

€€ VALERIUSSTRAAT 128 B
214 1075 GD, OUD-ZUID
T 676 46 47
WWW.RESTAURANT-
BOND.NL

OPEN LUNCH MON-FRI 11
AM-3 PM, DINNER DAILY
6-10.30 PM
RESERVATION REC.
SEATING: 54
GROUPS: MAX. 14
BAR

TERRACE
DOGS: PREFERABLY NOT
MUSIC: SOUL
AMBIENCE: MODERN

Soapies eat here, quality varies.

Herengracht

€€ HERENGRACHT 435
187 1017 BR, CENTRUM
T 616 24 82 / F 775 02 99
WWW.DEHERENGRACHT.NL

OPEN DAILY 11 AM-11 PM,
IN SUMMER AT 10 AM
RESERVATION REC.
SEATING: 74, CHEF'S
TABLE 19
GROUPS: MAX. 35
BAR

TERRACE AT THE WATER-
SIDE
PRIVATE DINING ROOMS:
ENTRESOL
MUSIC: BACKGROUND
AMBIENCE: LOUNGE

Noisy, modern lounge restaurant.

Supperclub

€€€ JONGE ROELENSTEEG 21
215 1012 PL, CENTRUM
T 344 64 00 / F 344 64 05
WWW.SUPPERCLUB.NL

OPEN DAILY 7 PM-1 AM
LOUNGE (FRI & SAT 7 PM-
3 AM)
RESERVATION ALWAYS
NEEDED
SEATING: 150
AIRCONDITIONING

CATERING: 'SUPPERCLUB
ON LOCATION'
NO DOGS
MUSIC: MIXED
AMBIENCE: EAT LYING
DOWN

Here cooking and eating are part of a theatrical setting.

VEGETARIAN

* Green Planet

€ SPUISTRAAT 122 A
216 1012 VA, CENTRUM
T 625 82 80
WWW.GREENPLANET.NL

OPEN 5.30-10.30 PM,
CLOSED SUN
RESERVATION REC.
SEATING: 30
GROUPS: MAX. 8
BAR
TERRACE
CASH PAYMENT ONLY

NO-SMOKING AREA AT
THE BAR
TAKEAWAY POSSIBLE
CATERING
MUSIC: JAZZ-REGGAE-
LOUNGE
AMBIENCE: SIMPLE

Excellent vegetarian restaurant.

** De Waaghals

€€ FRANS HALSSTRAAT 29
217 1072 BK, OUD-ZUID
T 679 96 09
WWW.WAAGHALS.NL

OPEN 5-9.30 PM,
CLOSED MON
RESERVATION REC.
SEATING: 42
GROUPS: MAX. 12
TERRACE

NO-SMOKING AREA
CATERING
NO CREDITCARDS
MUSIC: BACKGROUND
AMBIENCE: SIMPLE-
MODERN

Here vegetarian and mostly organic food is prepared by a collective.

Best Restaurants, Amsterdam centre

The numbers in the squares are referring to the list of Best Restaurants, page 79 ff.

©www.routecraft.com

CENTRAL
STATION

HET IJ

152
29
161
172
20
50
94
81
41
PR. HENDRIKKADE
OOSTERDOK
37
39
15
38
NIEUW-
MARKT
31 22
44 62
201
7
111
146 147
198
166
32
57
3
NDT-
N
110
144
75
26 116
115
25 143
179
93
24
194 123
103
AMSTEL
UTRECHTSE-
STRAAT
WEESPERSTRAAT
PLANTAGE MIDDENLAAN
SARPHATISTRAAT
MAURITSKADE
WIBAUTSTRAAT

Best Restaurants, Amsterdam

The numbers in the squares are referring to the list of Best Restaurants, page 79 ff.

INDEX

The numbers in the squares are referring to the list of Best Restaurants, page 79 ff. and the maps on page 120 ff.